HOW TO DRAW
SPORTS THINGS
for kids

ALLI KOCH

Paige Tate &co.

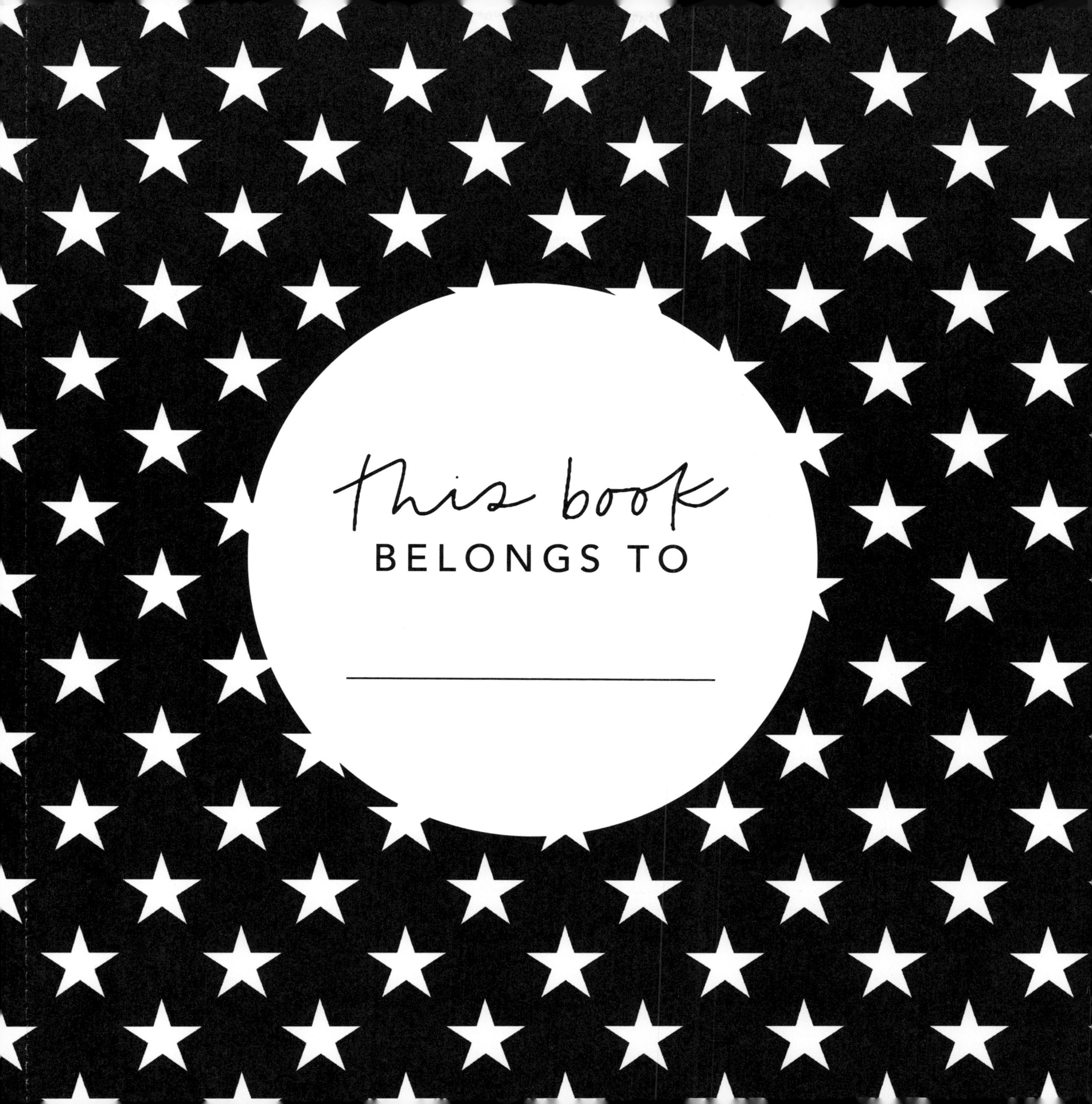
this book
BELONGS TO

LET'S DRAW!

The nice thing about being an artist is that you can make the rules. Everyone has their own style, which is why your drawings will look different from someone else's. In this book, each project is broken down into easy-to-follow steps. My goal is to help you see the simple parts of what may seem like a hard thing to draw.

We will start with the most basic outline or guide and work our way up. You will start to see a pattern with each sports thing we draw, starting with simple guidelines, then breaking down "C" and "S" shaped lines, and lastly erasing the unneeded lines for the finished look. Don't forget to draw your lines lightly first so it is easier to erase them. My favorite thing to say when drawing is:

If it was perfect, it would not look handmade!

I cannot wait for you to get started.
Happy drawing!

TOOLS

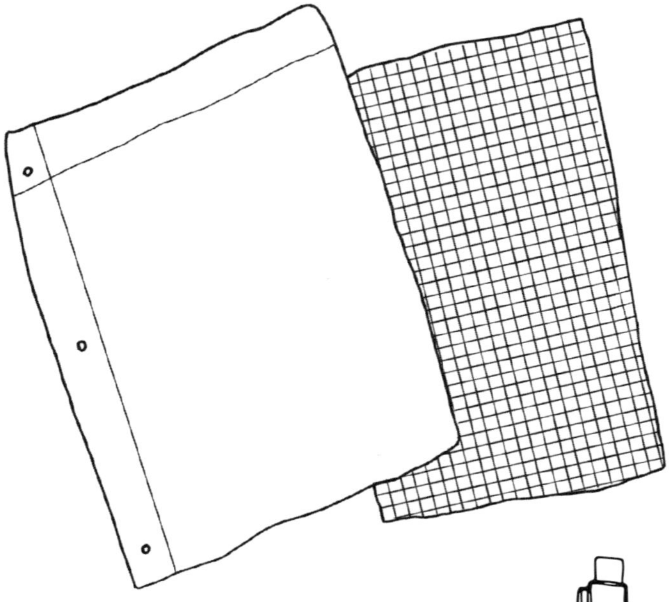

The cool thing about art is that you can use any tool you want! Yep, that's right! You are the artist, so feel free to be creative. For this book, let's keep it simple. It's easy to learn using either blank sheets of paper or grid paper.

When you are learning to draw, you really only need a pencil and a good eraser. To follow the step-by-step instructions, draw everything lightly, then go over your lines with whatever tool you would like to use. You could use different pens, markers, colored pencils, or even crayons to add details to your drawings.

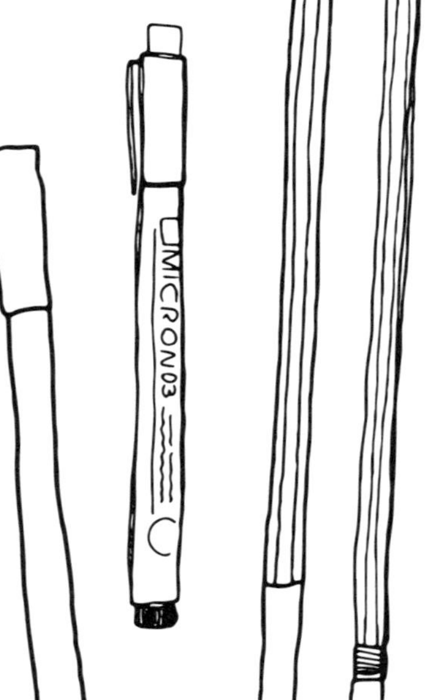

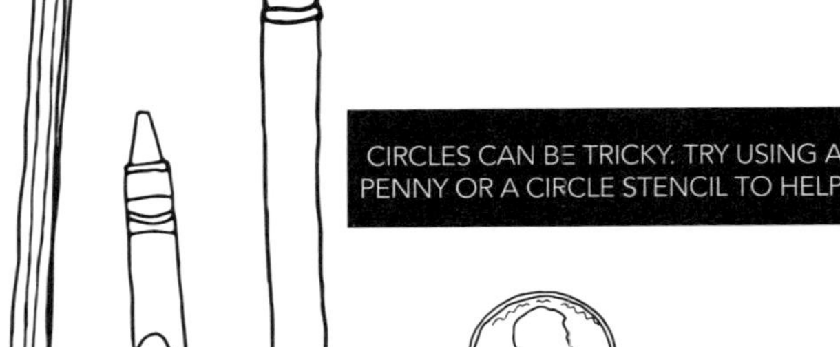

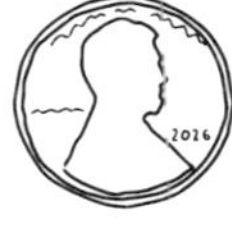

BREAK IT DOWN

Anyone can draw! If you can write your ABCs (which I am pretty sure you can do!), then you can draw everything in this book. Each project can be broken down into a bunch of "C" and "S" shaped lines. Almost anything that is round is two simple "C" shaped lines put together. An "S" shaped line is for when something has a dip or curvy line.

Most of the projects in this book are broken down into six or eight steps. What you need to draw in each step will appear as a black line; what you have already drawn will appear as gray lines. There are more than 40 sports-themed illustrations in this book for you to learn how to draw. The chapter dividers in this book are also bonus coloring pages that you can color!

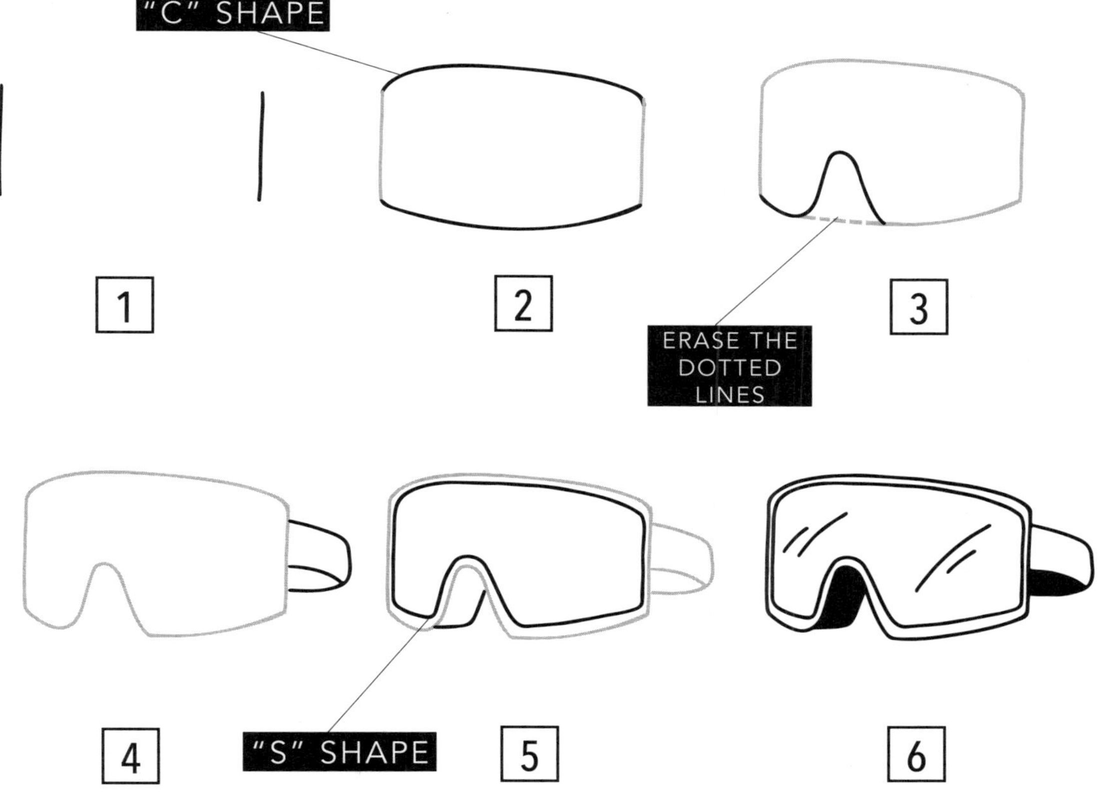

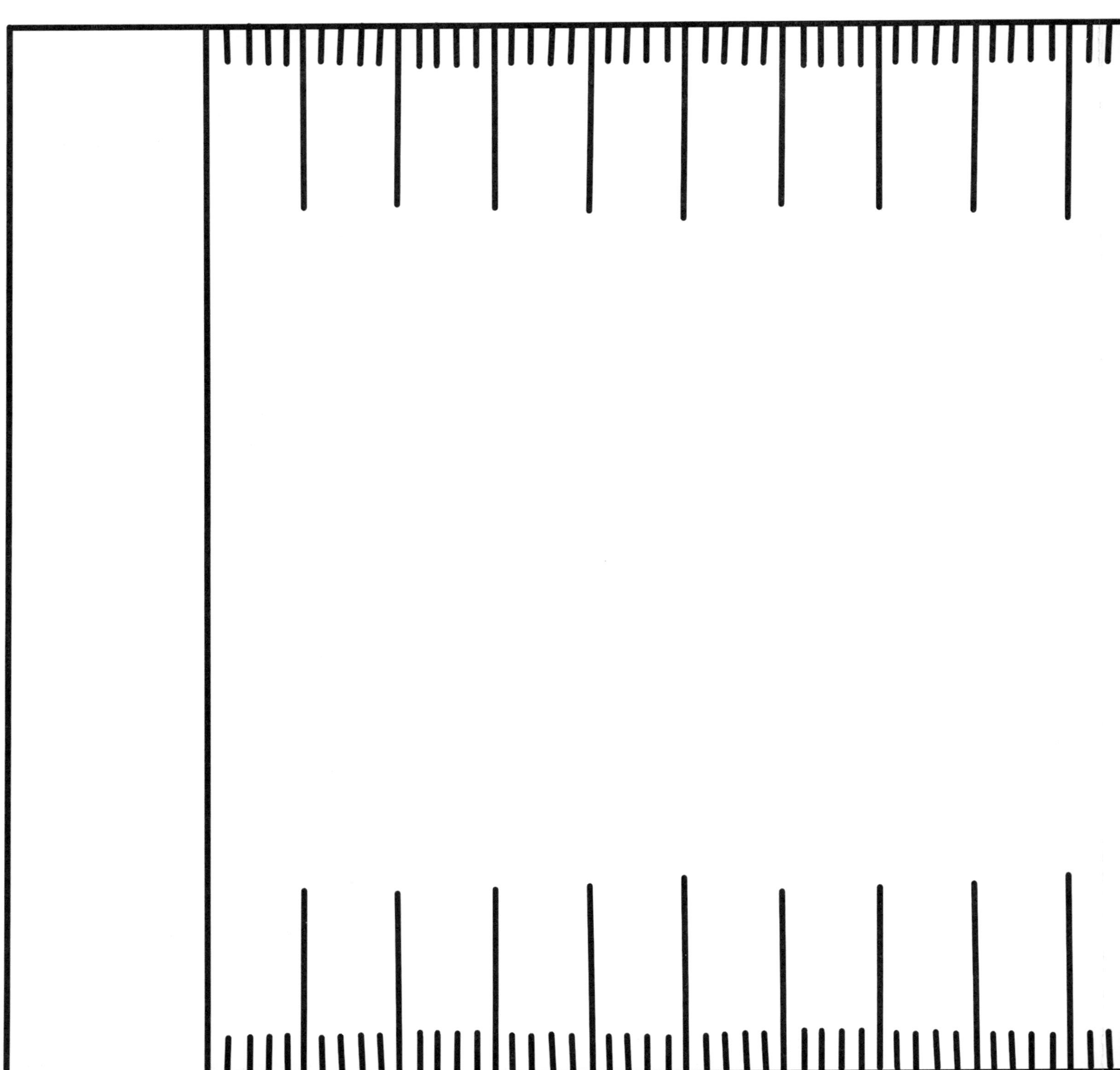

GAME GEAR

FOOTBALL

Footballs are nicknamed *pigskins*, but they're actually made
of cowhide or synthetic leather today.

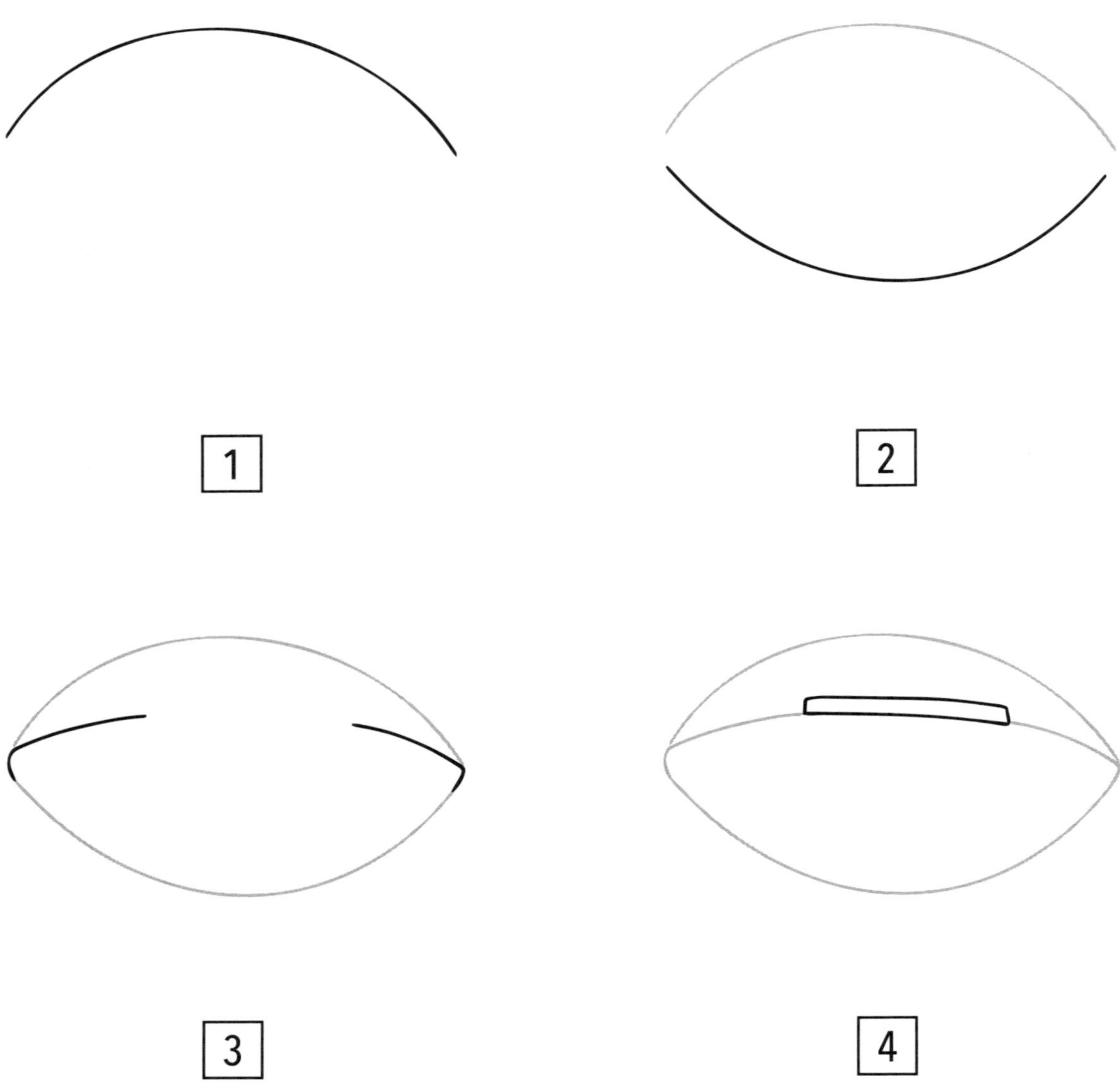

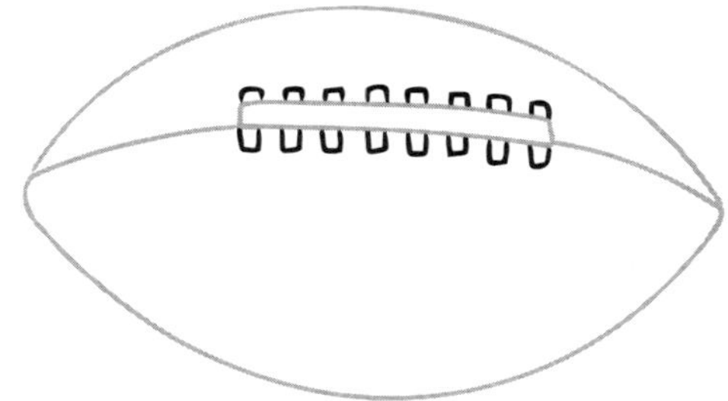

5

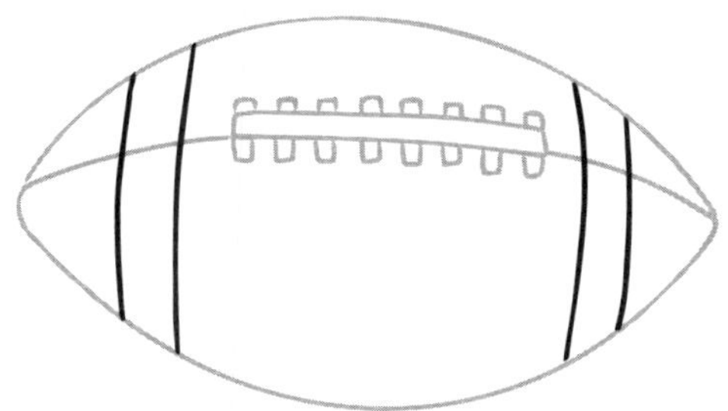

6

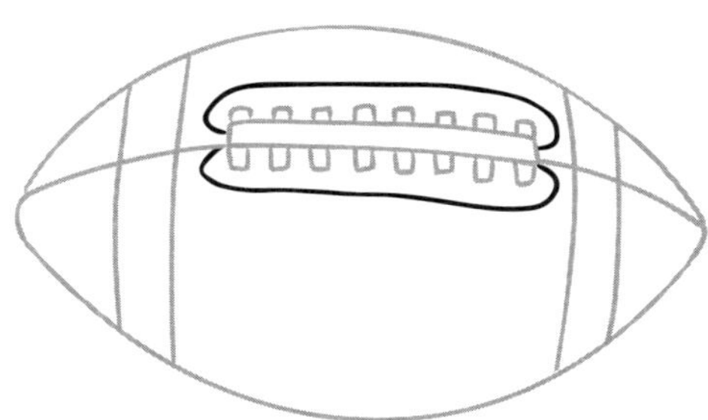

7

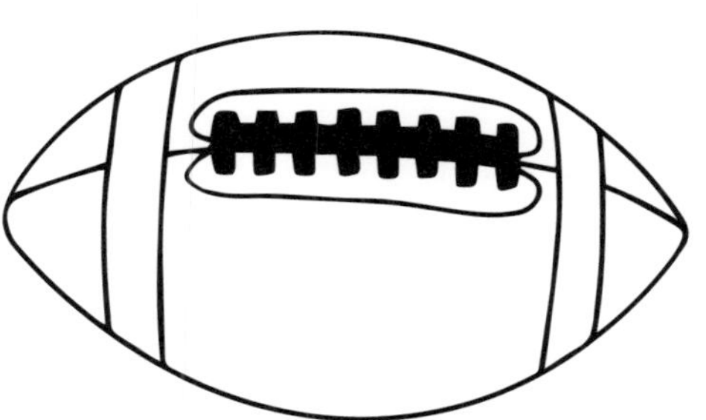

8

FOOTBALL HELMET

Professional football helmets have built-in speakers so quarterbacks can hear plays from coaches on the sidelines.

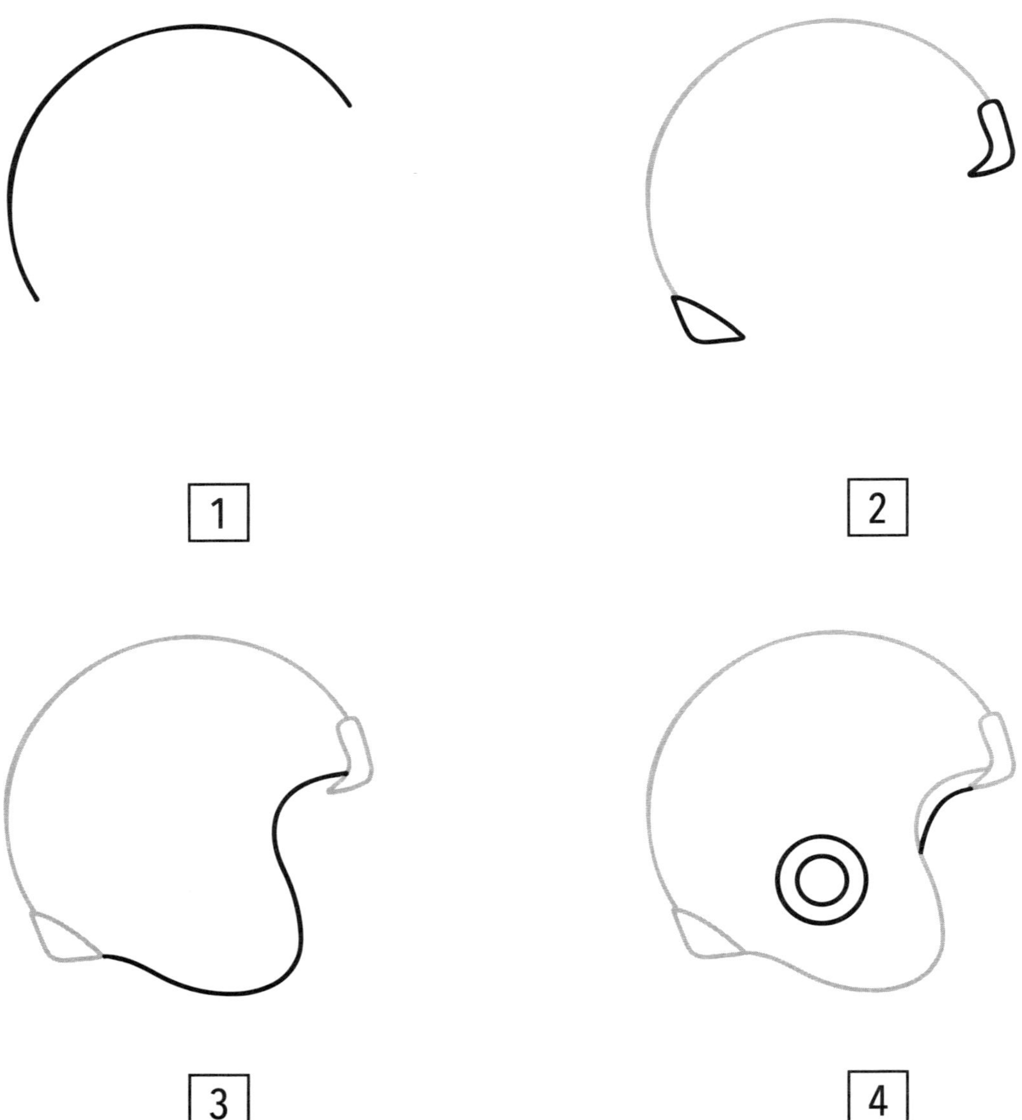

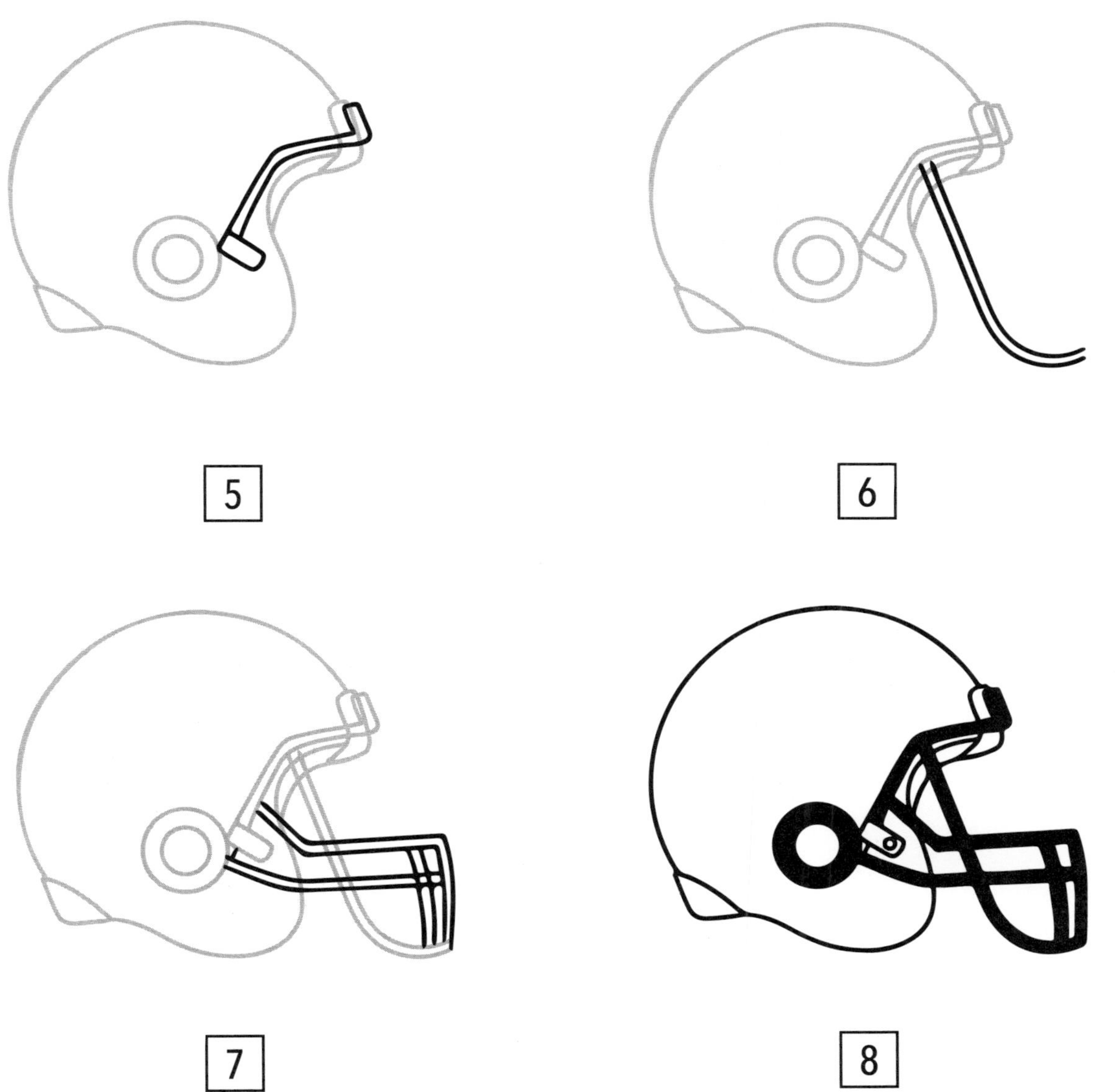

5
6
7
8

VOLLEYBALL

Volleyball was invented in 1895 as a mix between basketball, tennis, and handball, and it was originally called *mintonette*.

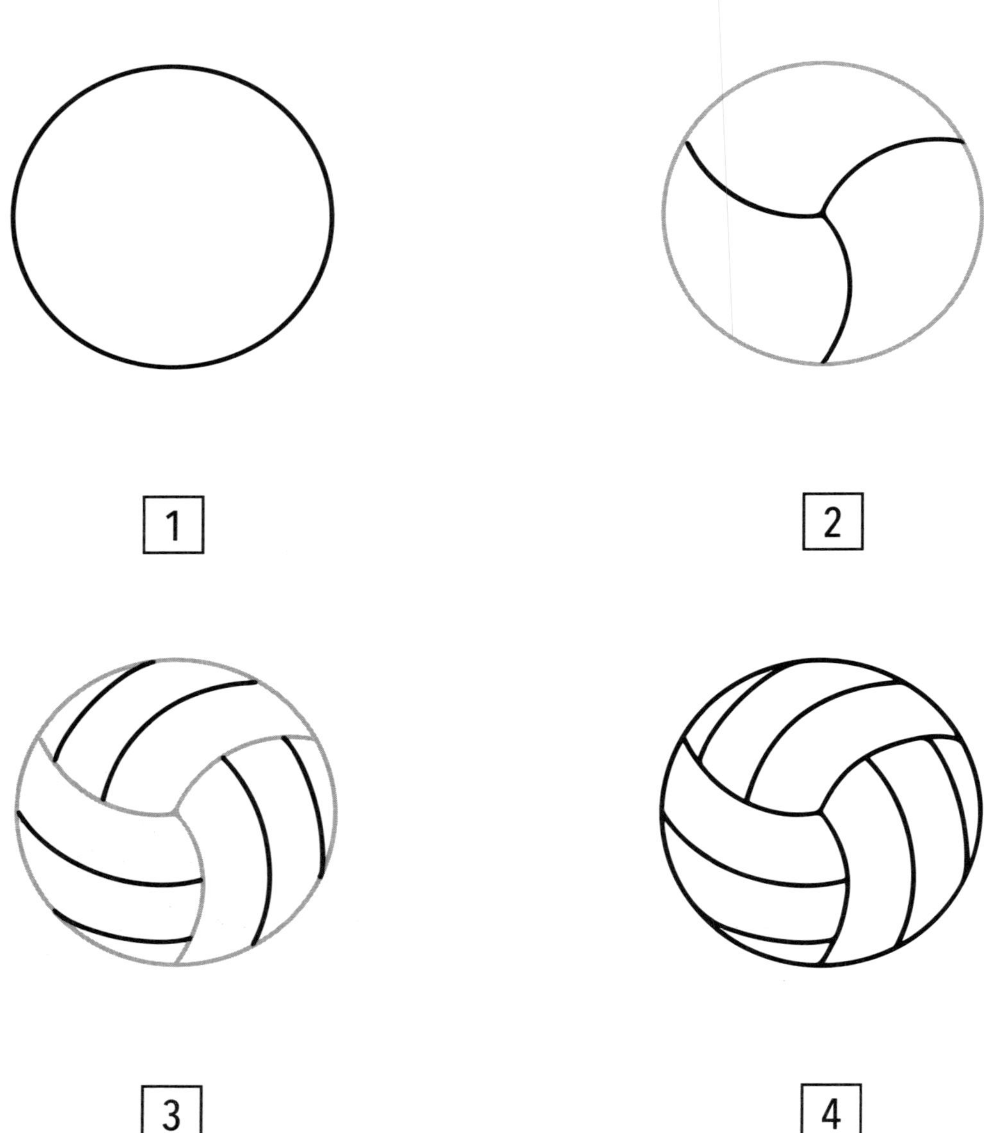

VOLLEYBALL NET

The fastest recorded volleyball spike in the Olympics hit 80 miles per hour—faster than most cars on the highway!

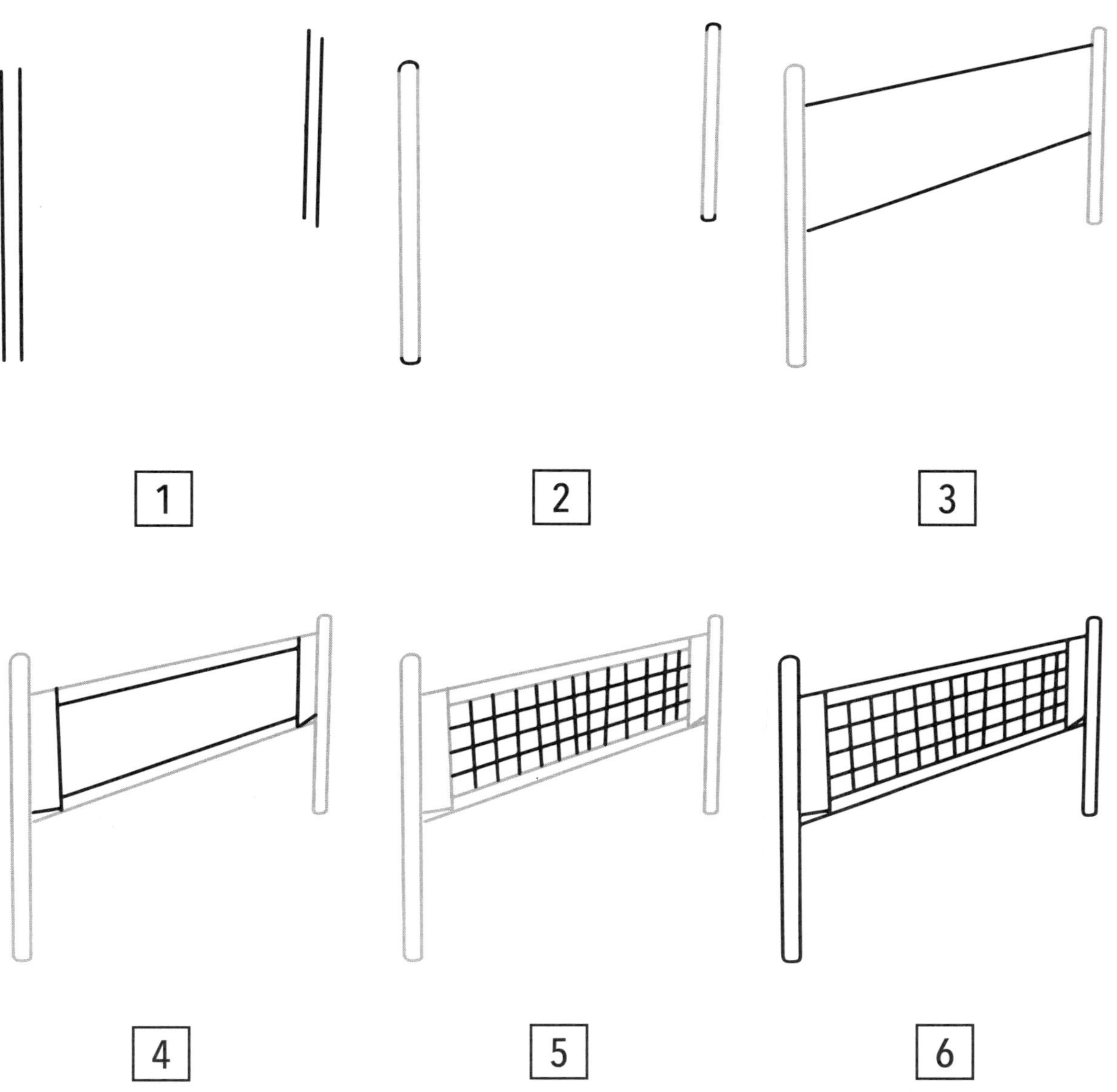

SOCCER BALL

A classic black-and-white soccer ball has 32 panels—
20 white hexagons and 12 black pentagons.

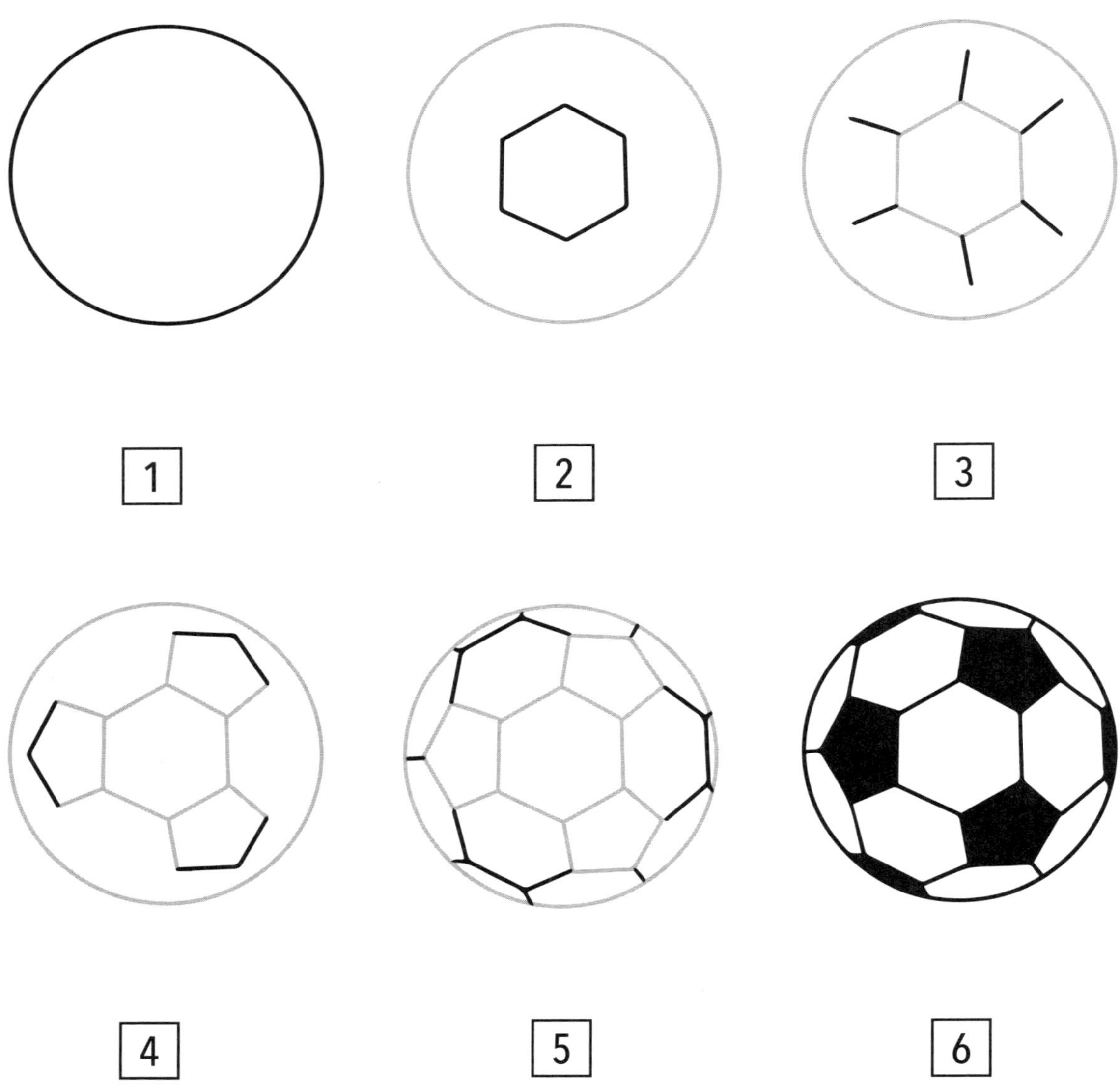

SOCCER GOAL

Soccer is the most popular sport in the world, played by over 250 million people across more than 200 countries.

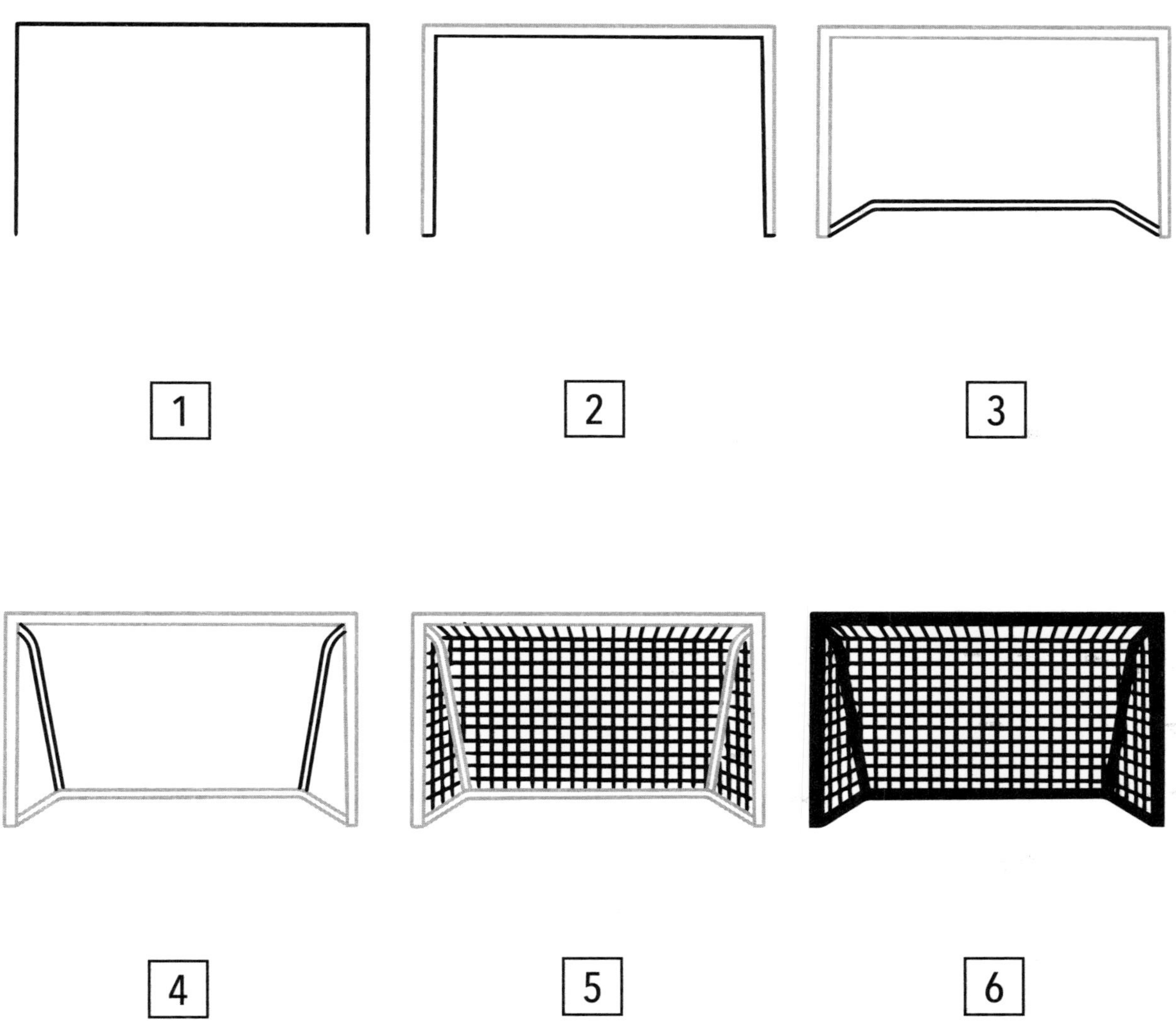

SOCCER CLEATS

There is no rule that a soccer player must wear cleats, only that they must have shoes on.

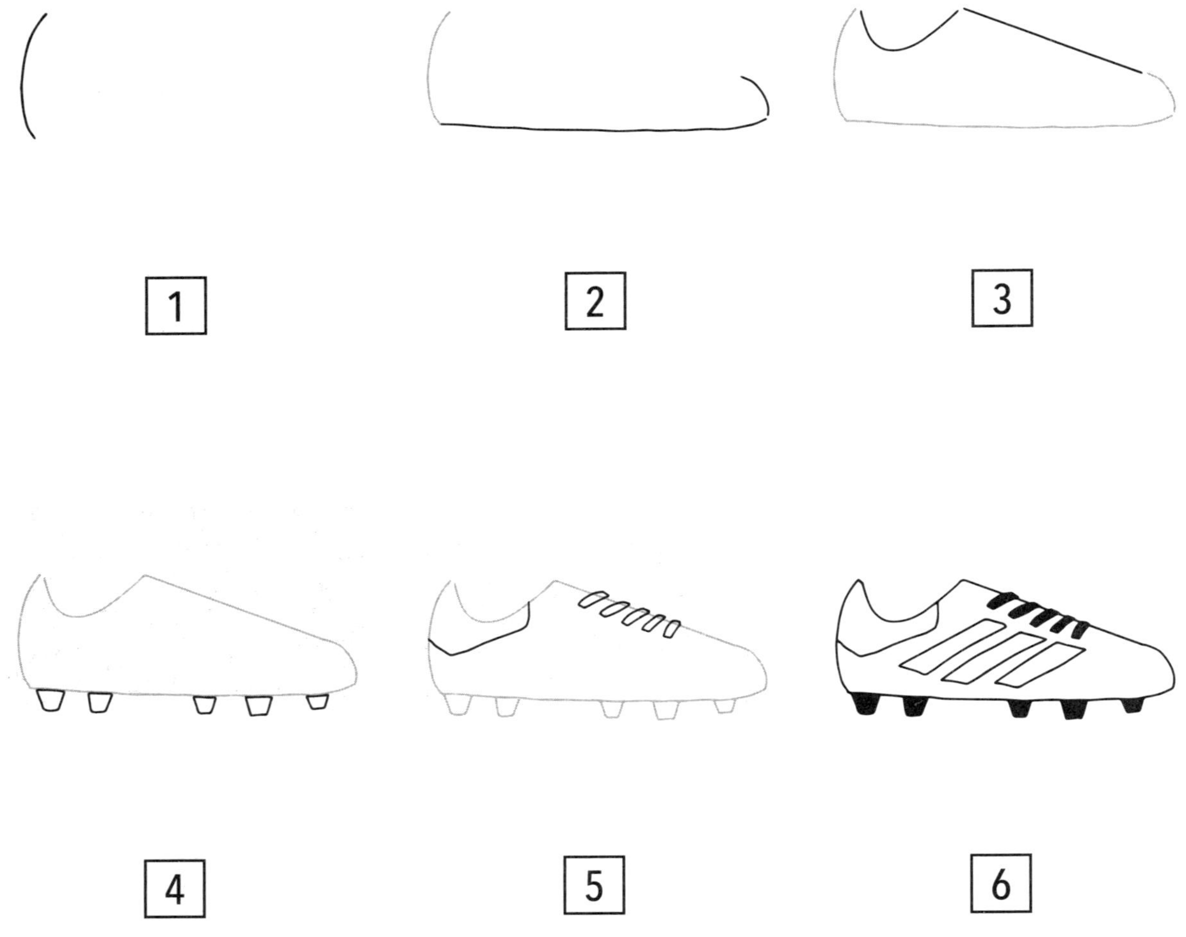

FIELD HOCKEY STICK

In field hockey, the action of moving the ball down
the field with the stick is called *dribbling.*

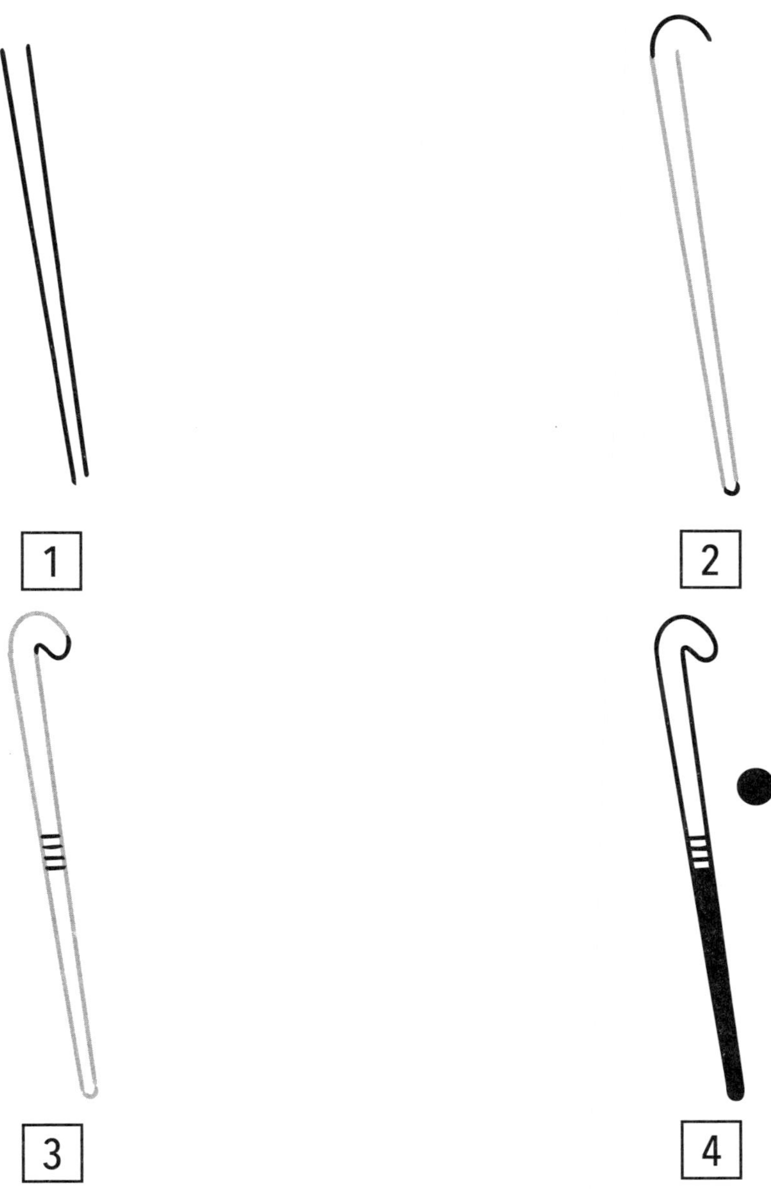

BASKETBALL

A regulation basketball has over 35,000 tiny dots to help players grip the ball.

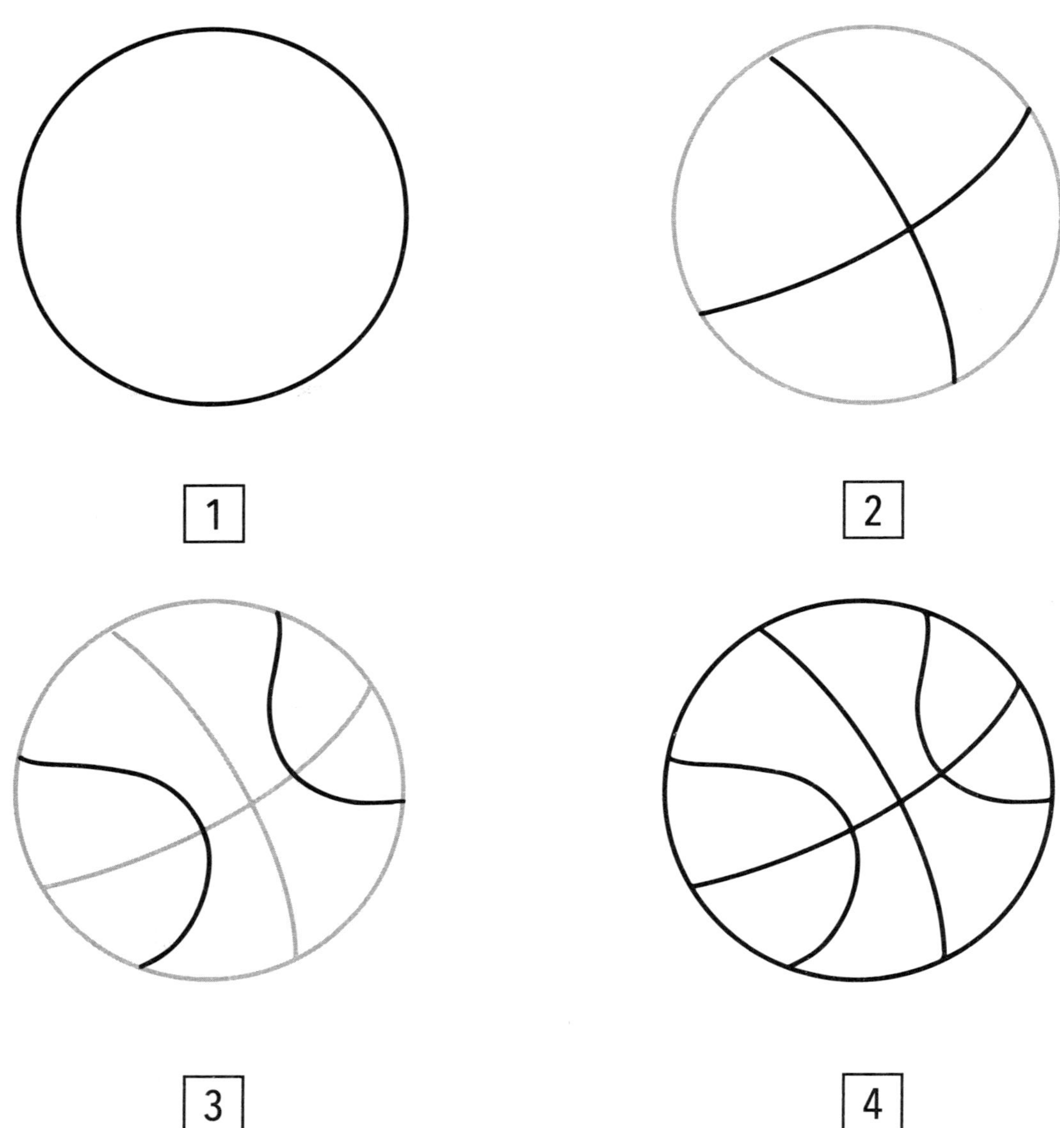

BASKETBALL HOOP

The first basketball hoop was just a peach basket nailed to a gym wall with no hole in the bottom.
Players had to fish the ball out after every shot.

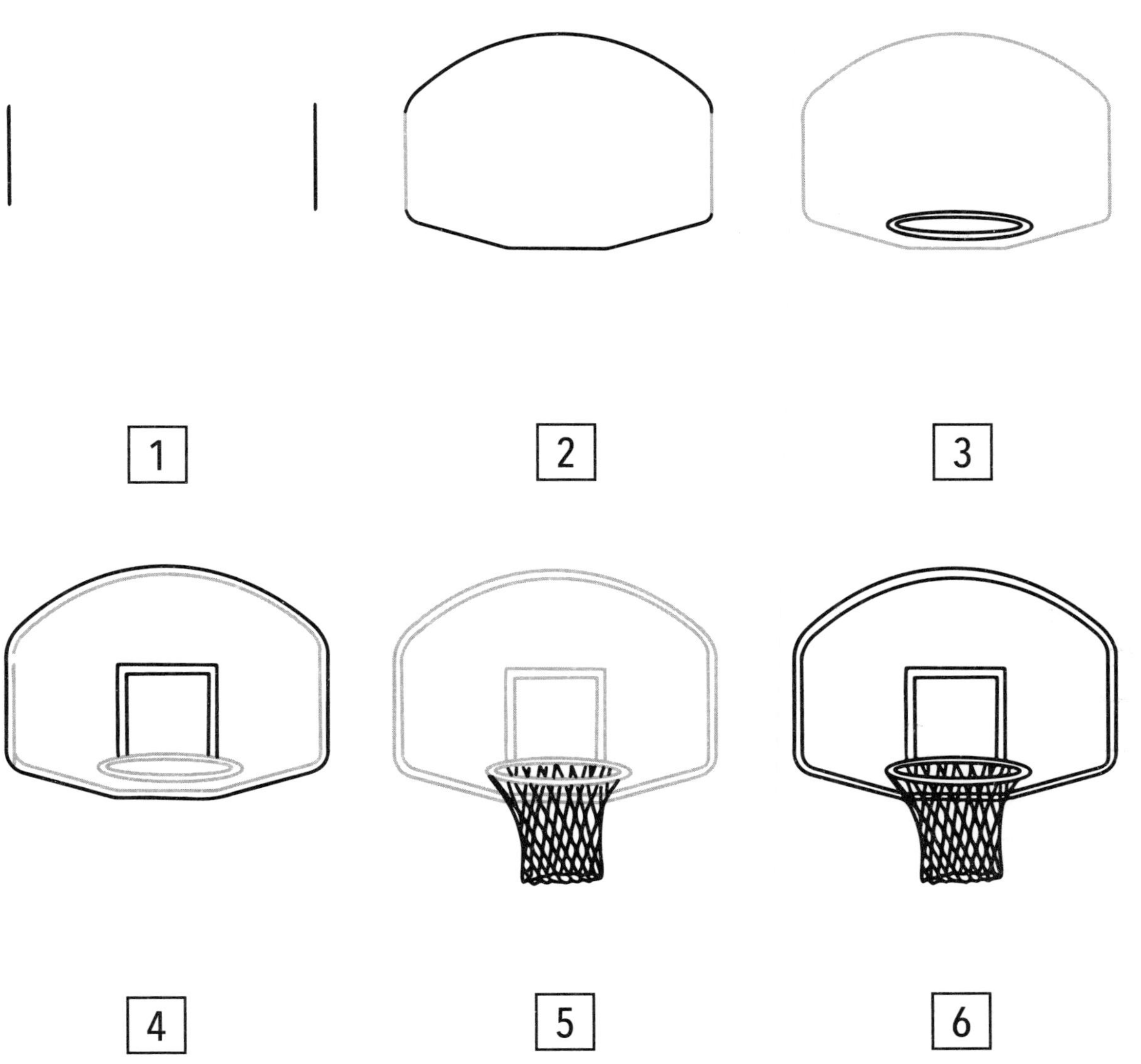

HOCKEY STICK

Early hockey sticks were carved from a single piece of wood and didn't have the bend you see in modern sticks.

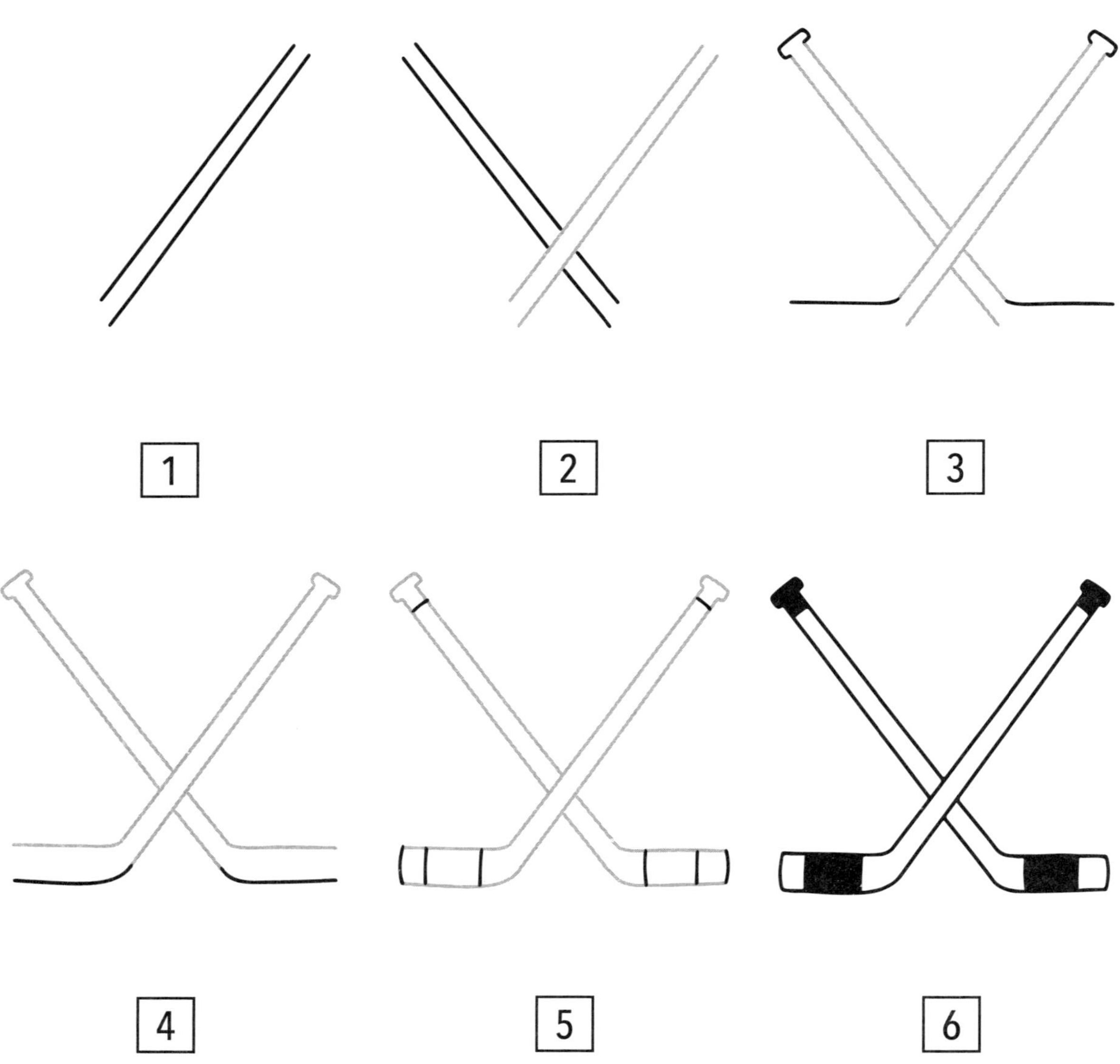

HOCKEY PUCK

Hockey pucks are frozen before games so they bounce less on the ice.

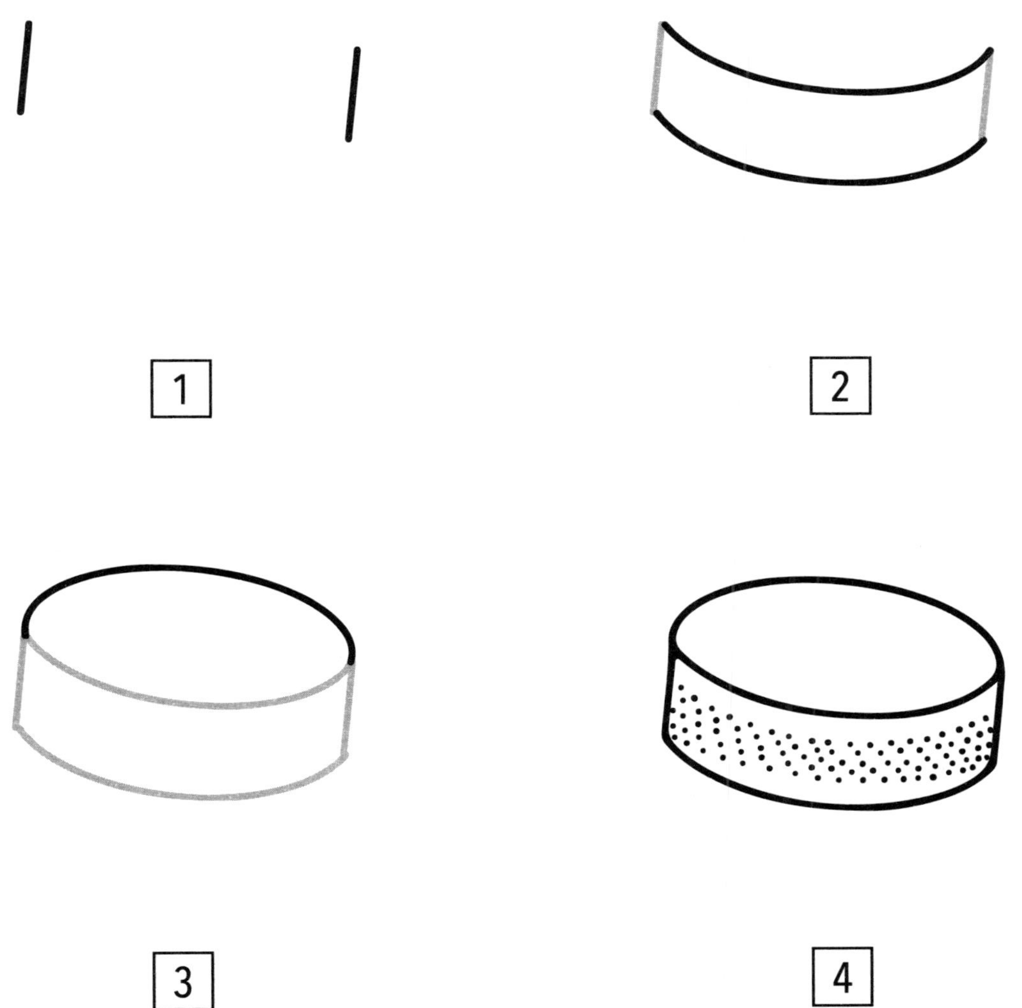

HOCKEY SKATES

The first hockey skates were made by attaching animal bones to boots with leather straps—no metal blades at all.

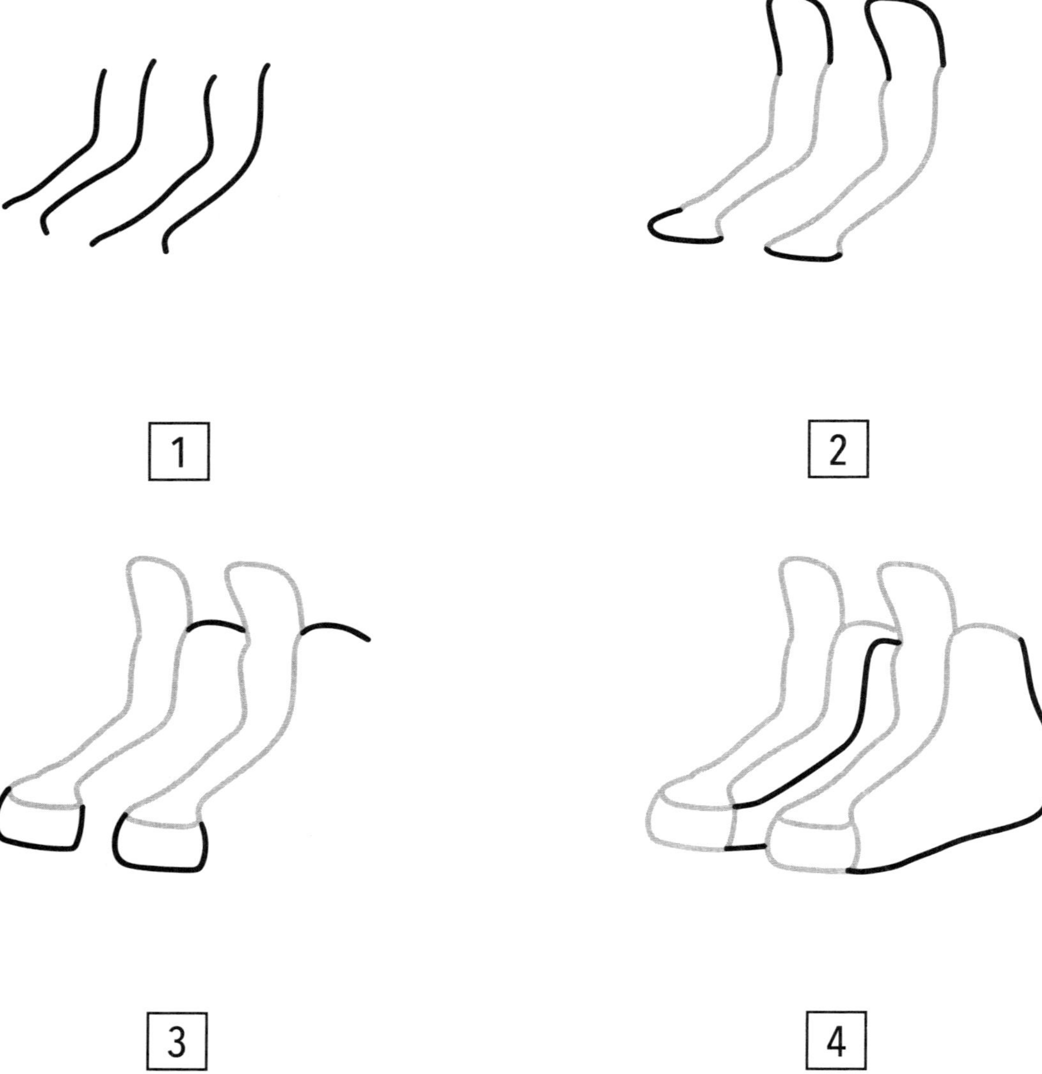

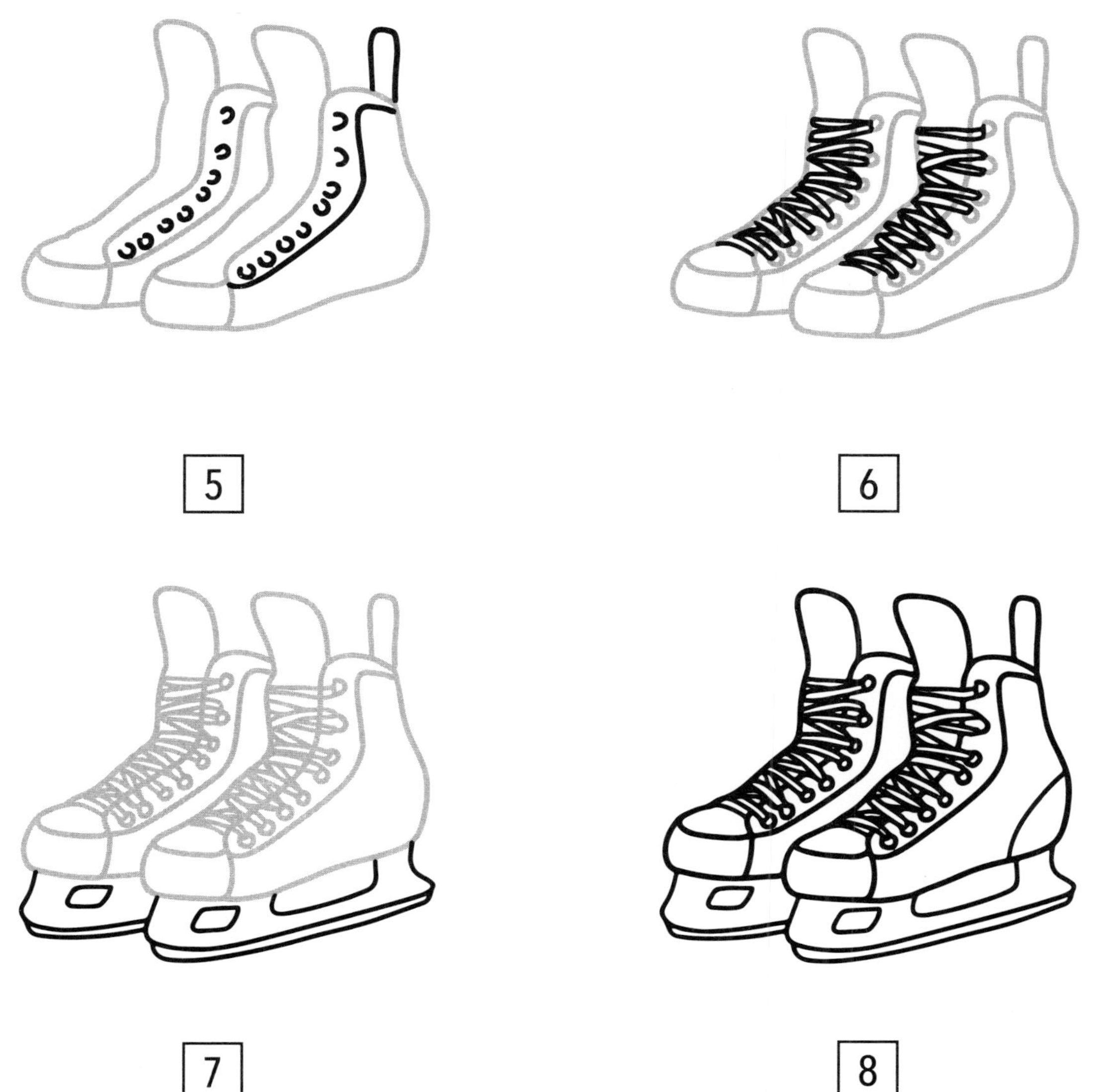

5
6
7
8

FIGURE SKATES

Unlike hockey skates, figure skates have a jagged edge at the front called a *toe pick* that helps skaters launch into jumps and land gracefully on the ice.

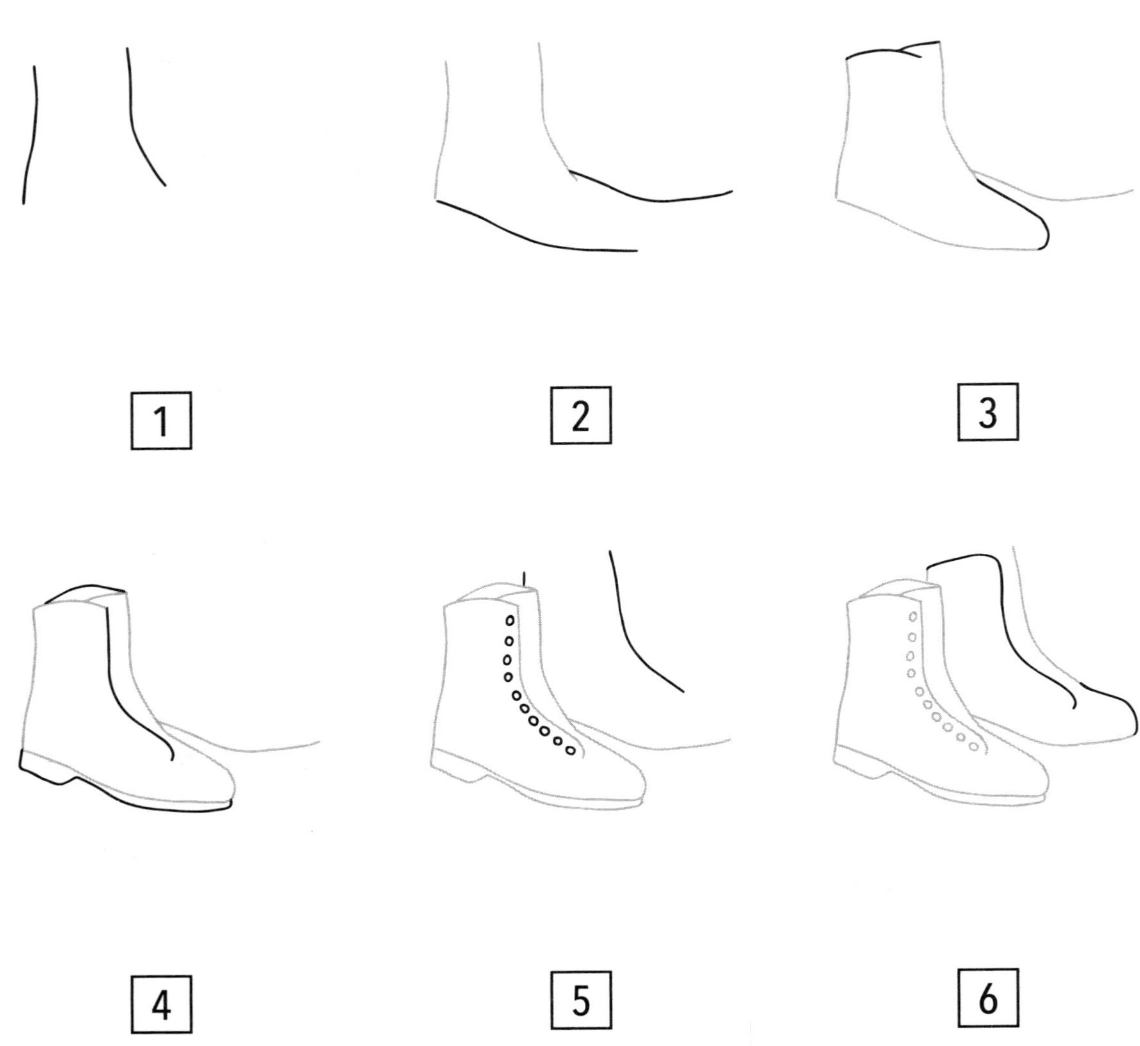

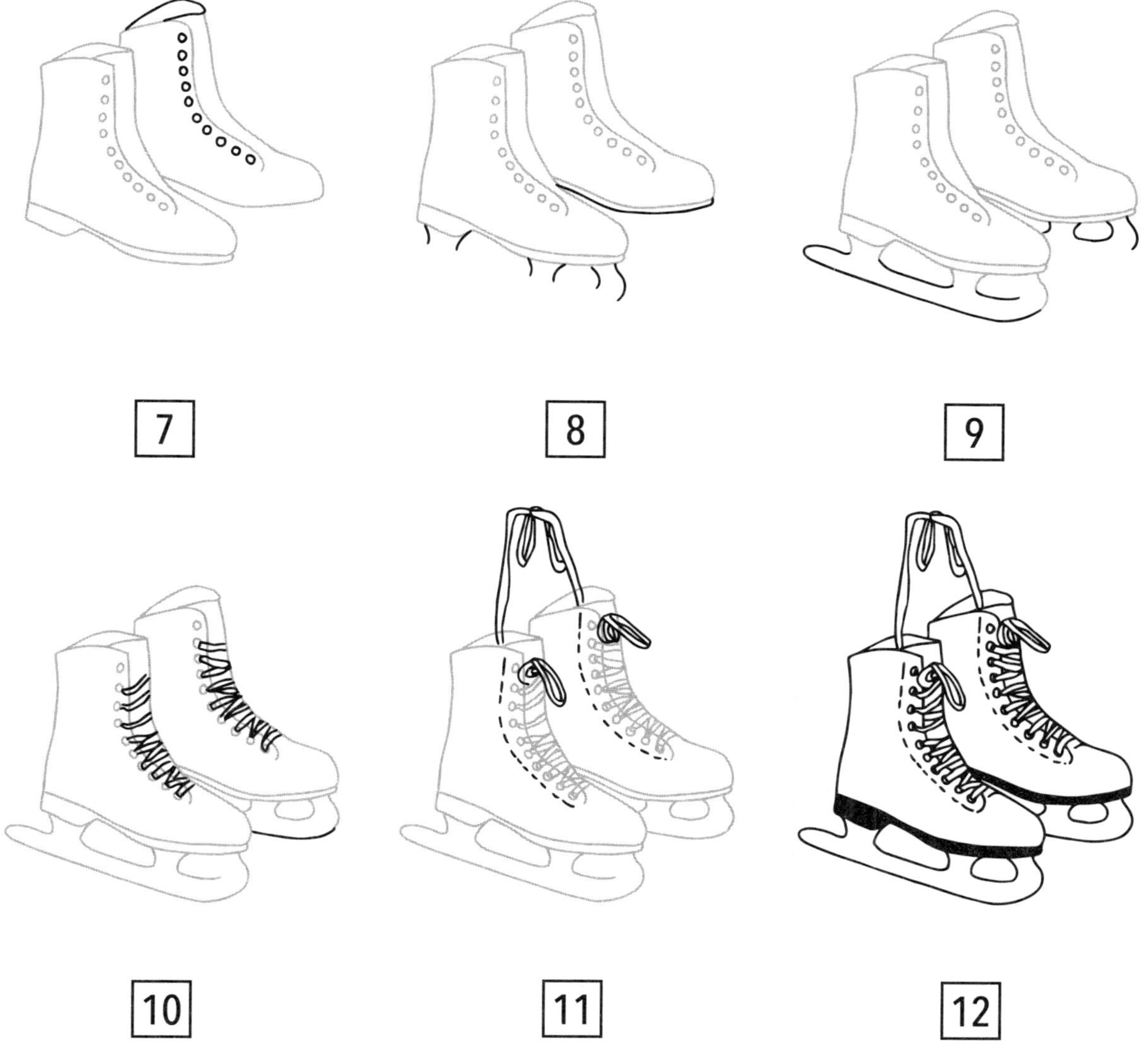

7
8
9
10
11
12

LACROSSE STICK

Lacrosse is one of the oldest team sports in North America.
It was invented by Indigenous tribes over 1,000 years ago.

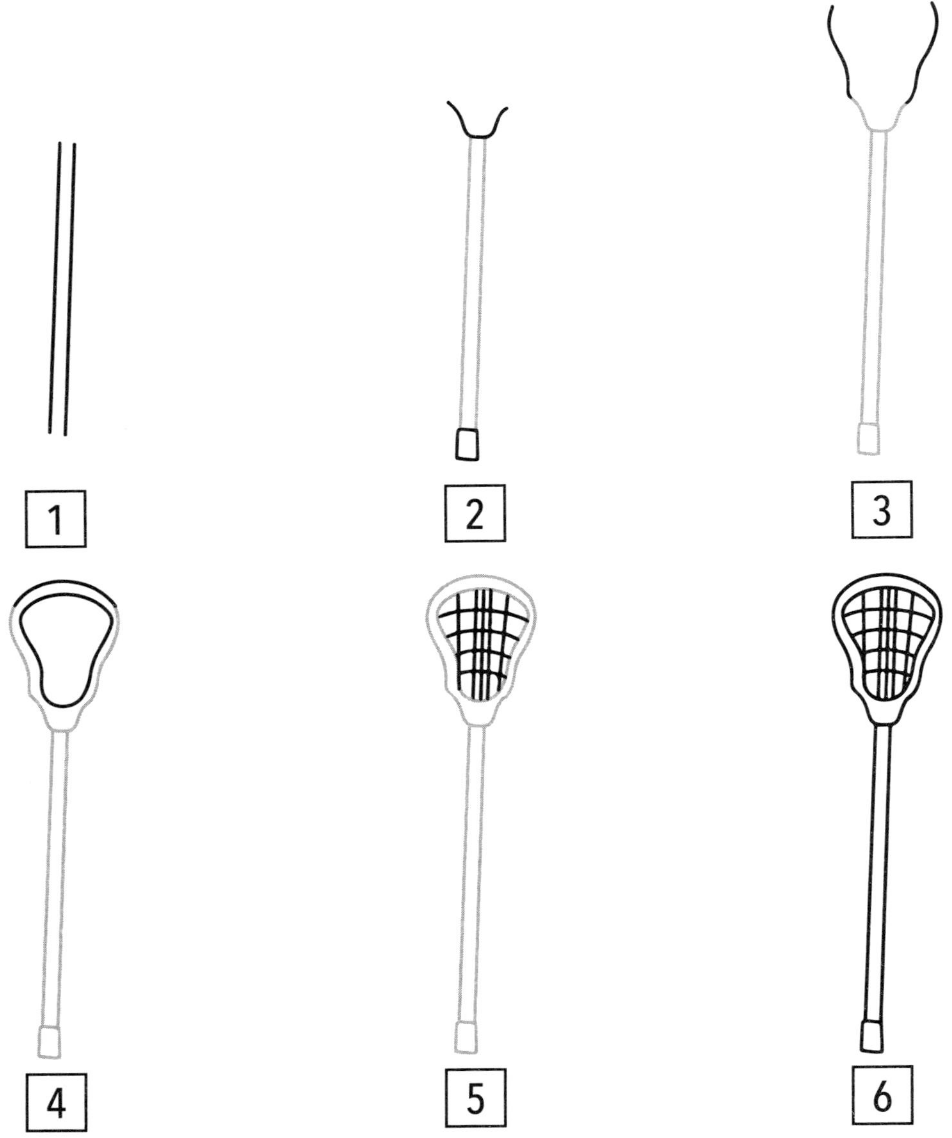

LACROSSE HELMET

A lacrosse ball can travel up to 100 miles per hour, making helmets necessary for safety.

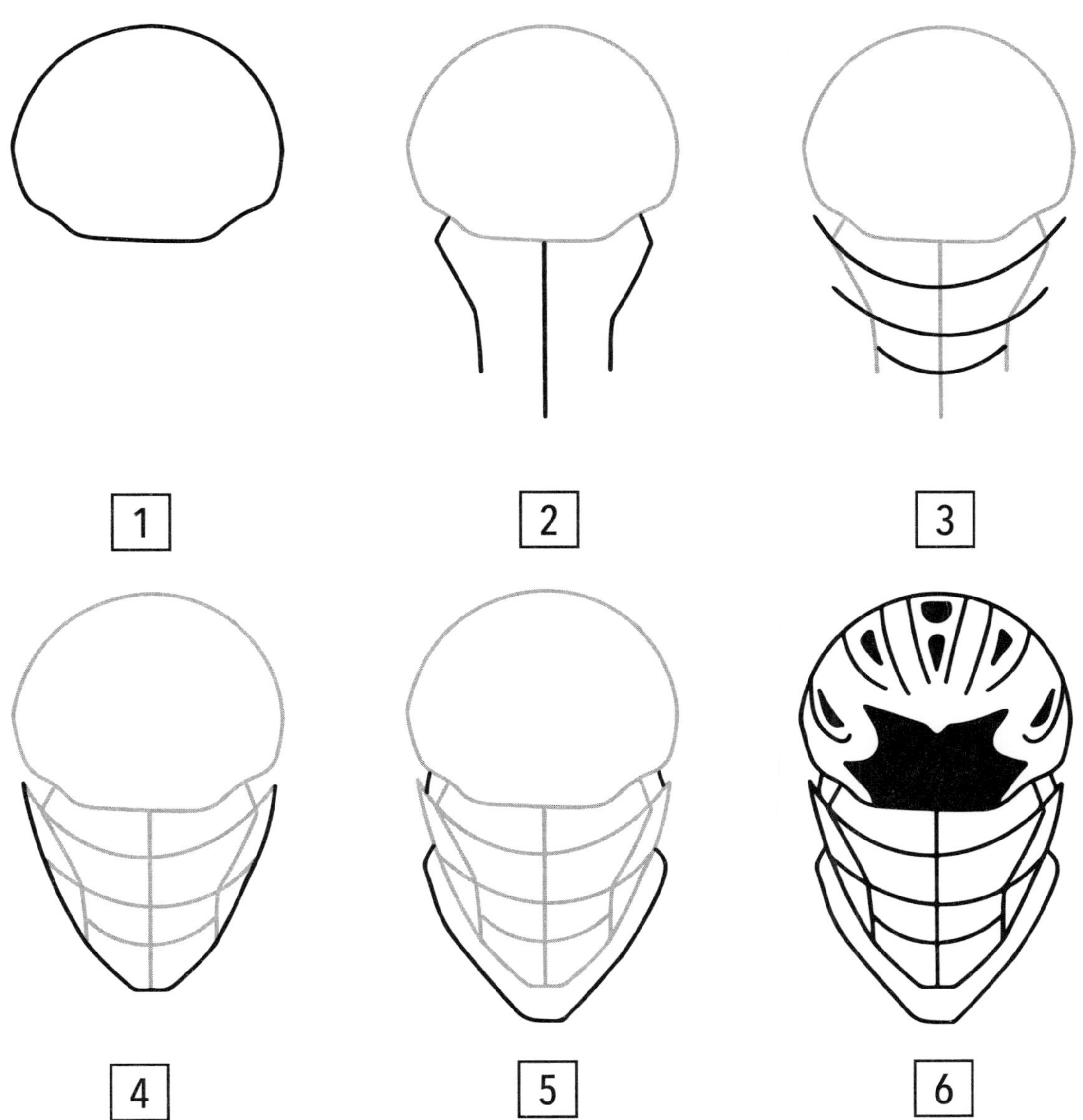

SNOWBOARD

Snowboards were originally called *snurfers* because the sport was inspired by surfing and skateboarding.

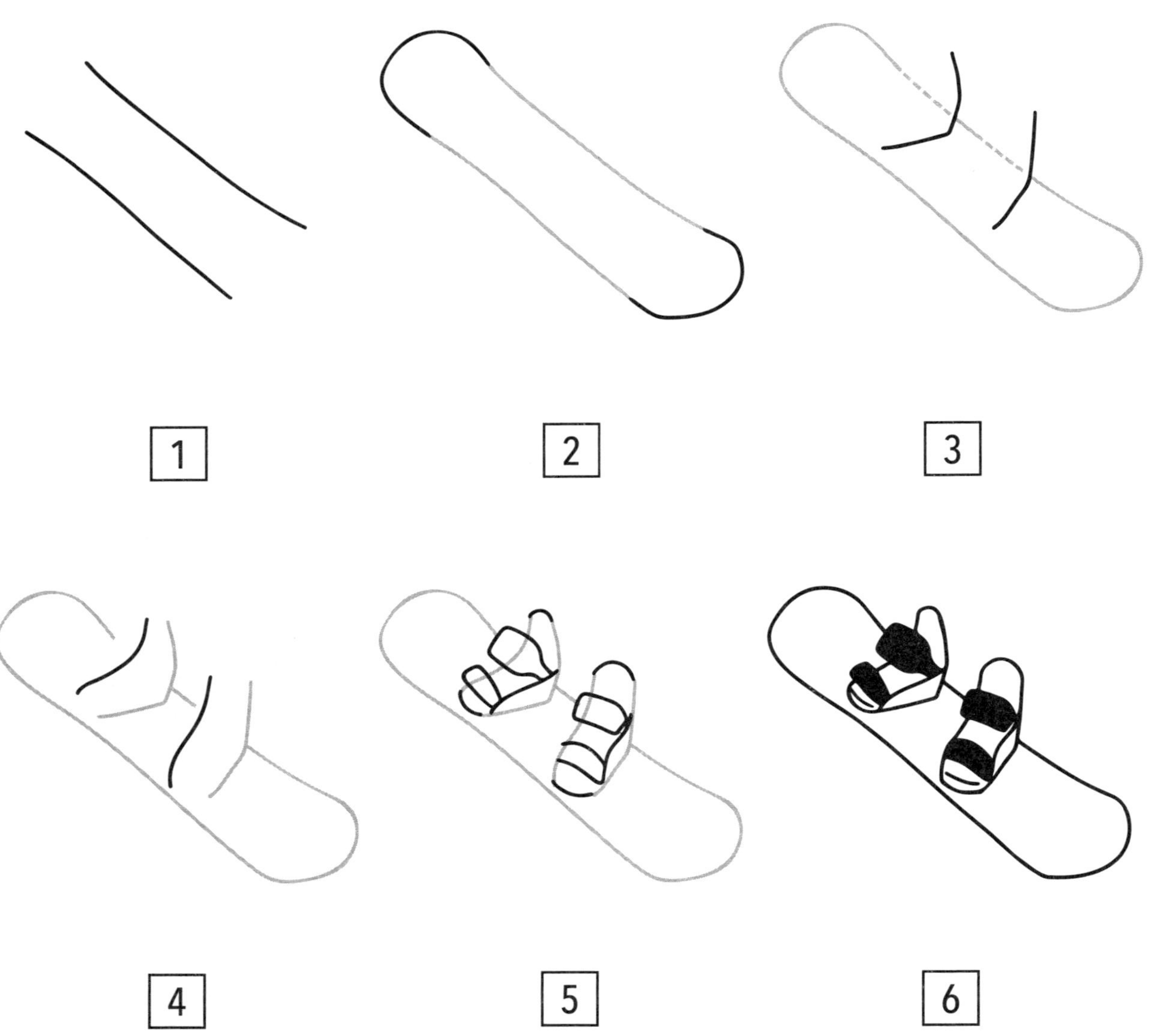

SNOW SKIS

The oldest known snow skis are over 8,000 years old and were found in Russia. Ancient humans used them to travel across the snowy land.

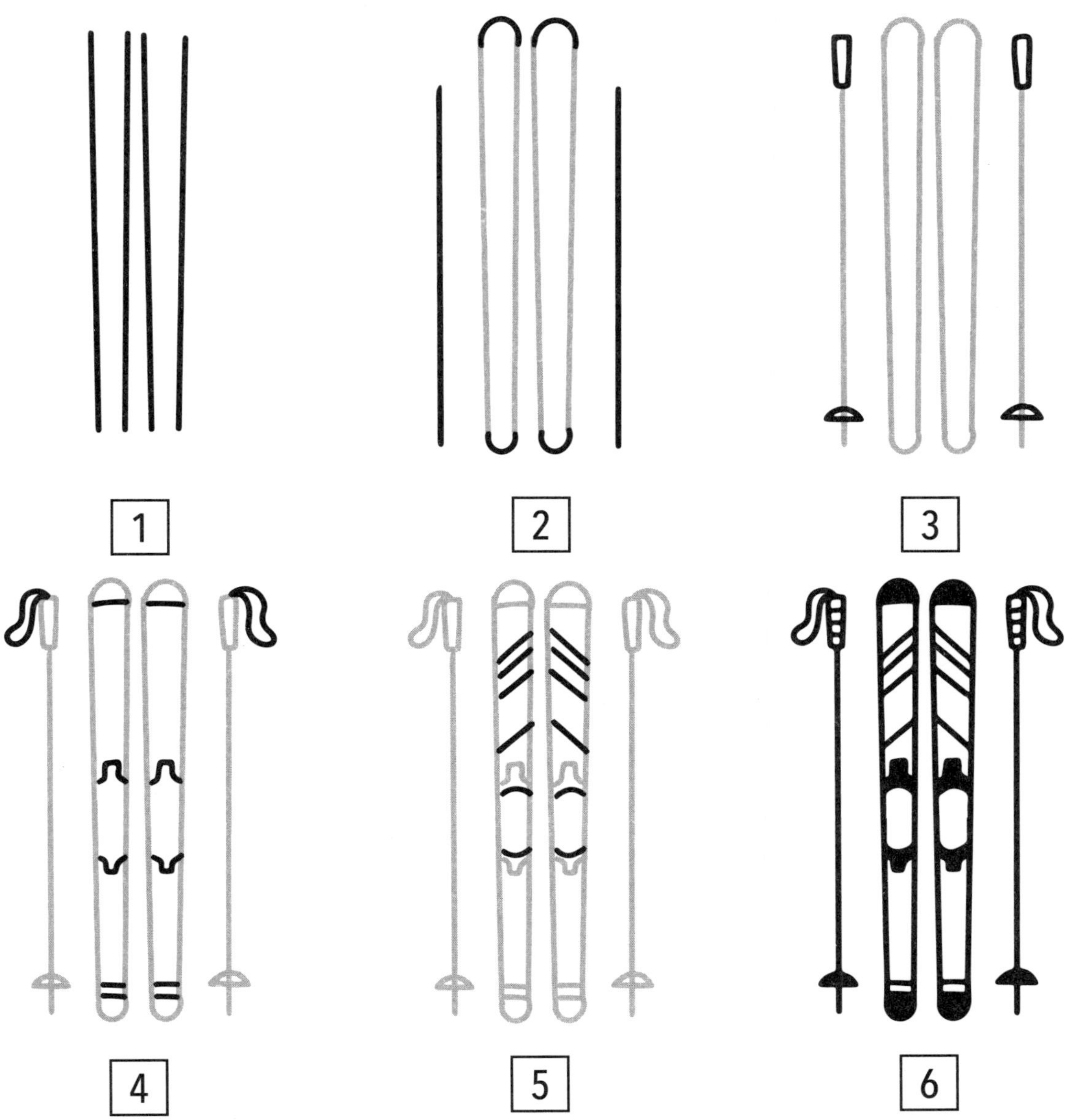

BOWLING BALL

Most bowling balls have three finger holes but some pro bowlers only use two for a better spin.

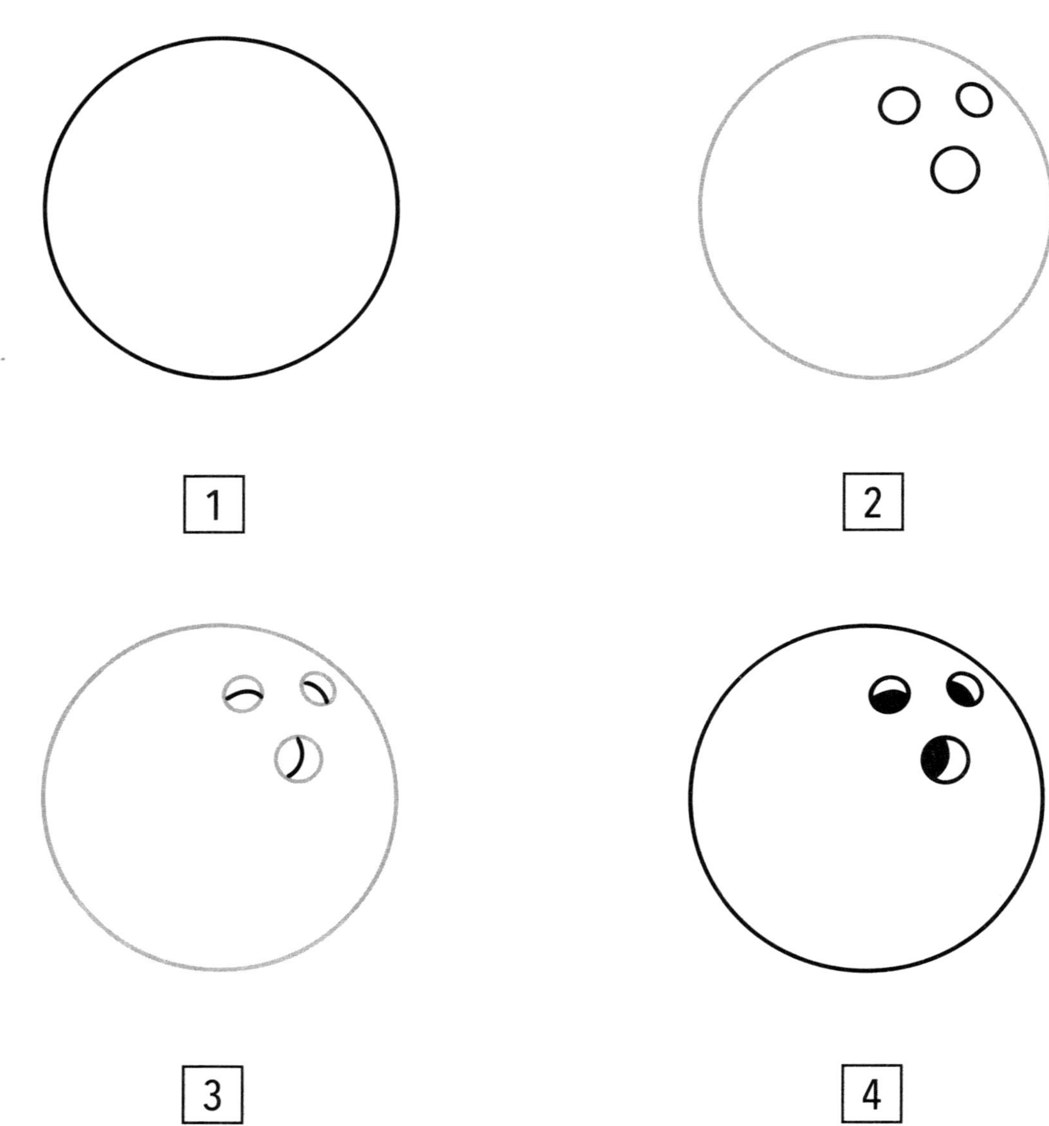

BOWLING PINS

Bowling pins are made from maple wood and are coated in plastic
so they can handle being hit again and again.

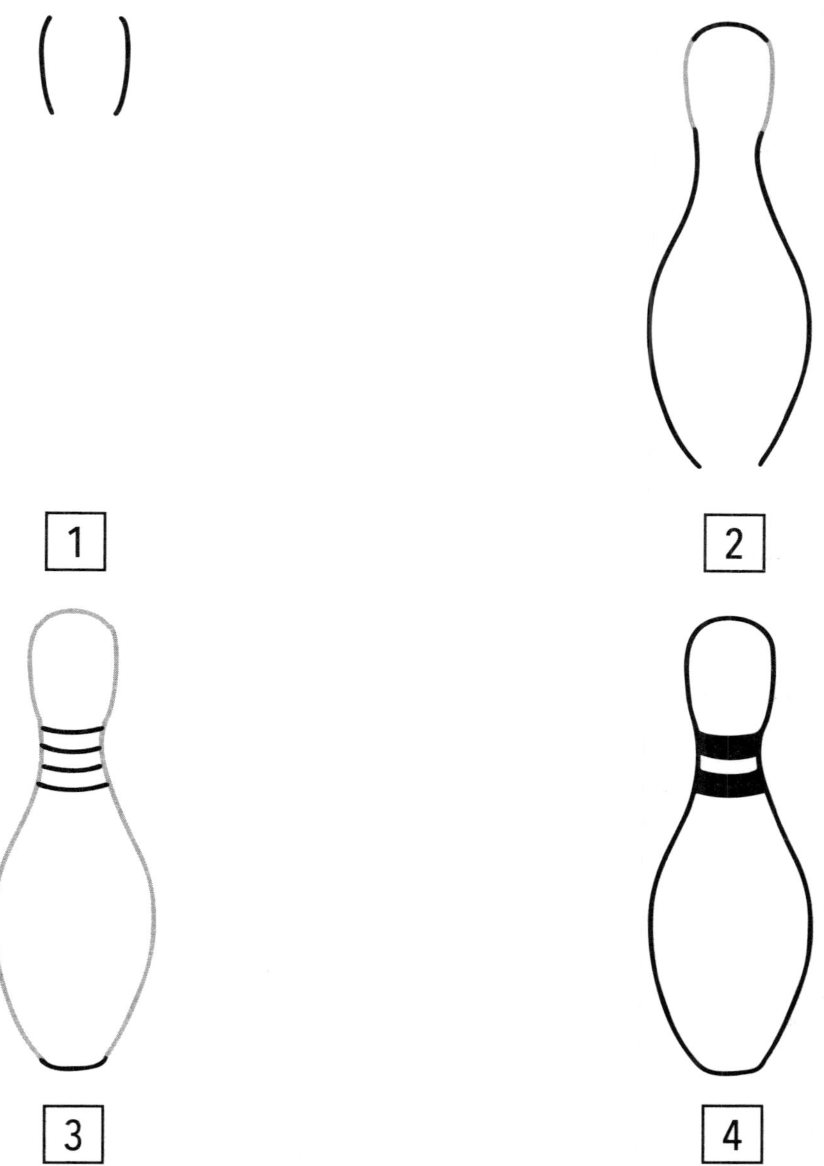

BOXING GLOVES

Boxers use different gloves for each part of training—bag gloves, sparring gloves, and fight gloves. Each one's built for power, speed, or safety.

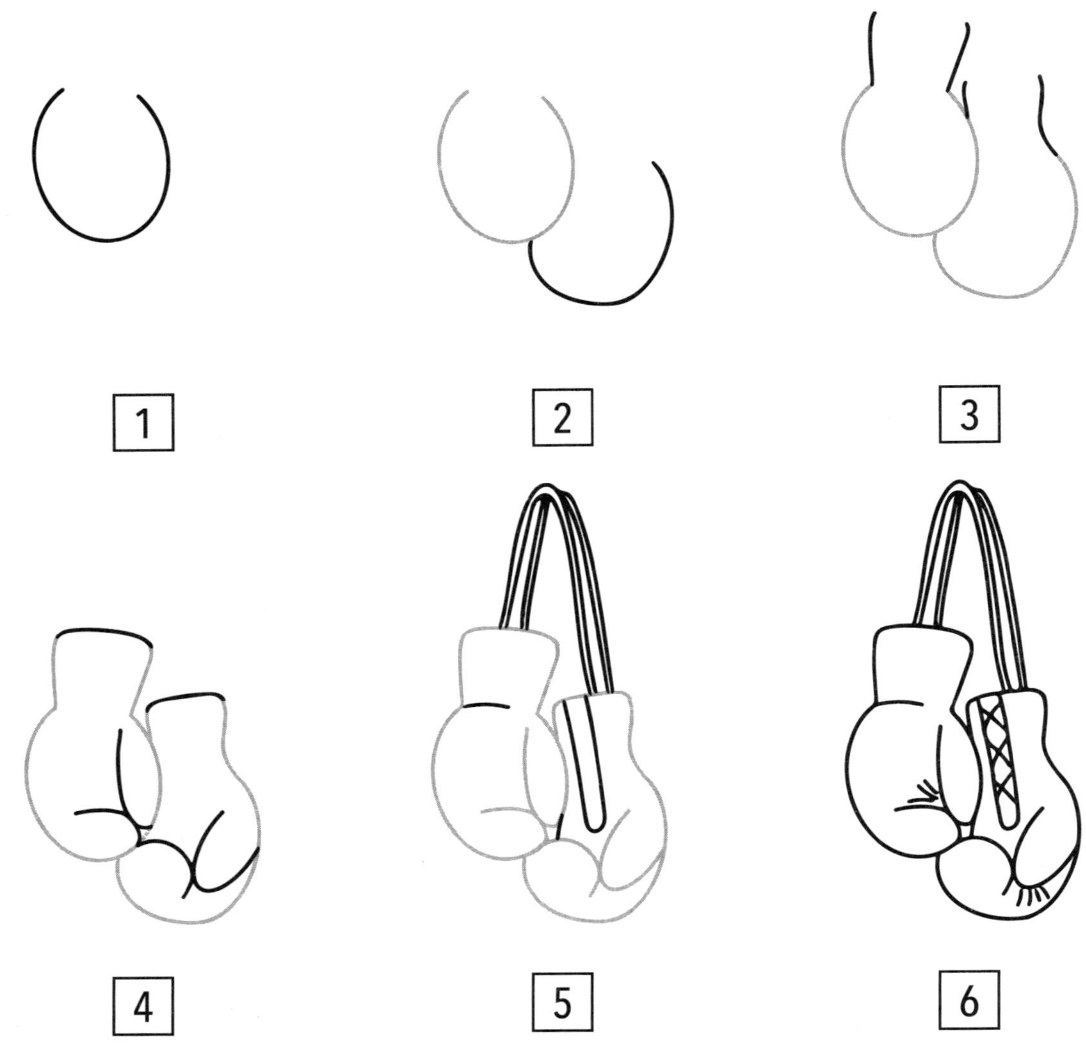

KARATE BELT

Karate belts show your rank—white means beginner, black means expert. In American karate, some schools use up to ten colors to track progress and keep kids motivated.

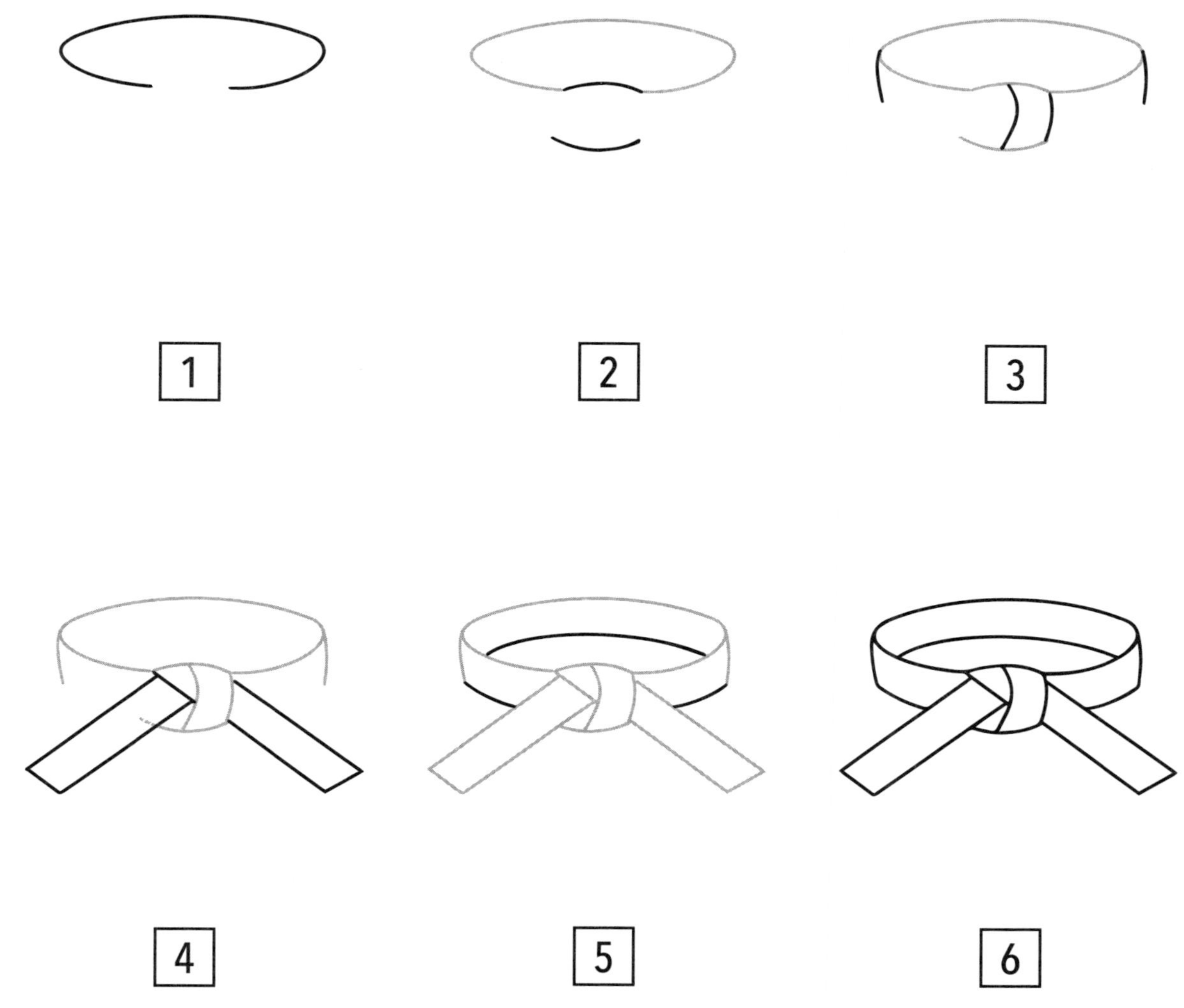

GOLF BALL

The tiny dimples on a golf ball help it fly farther by reducing air resistance.

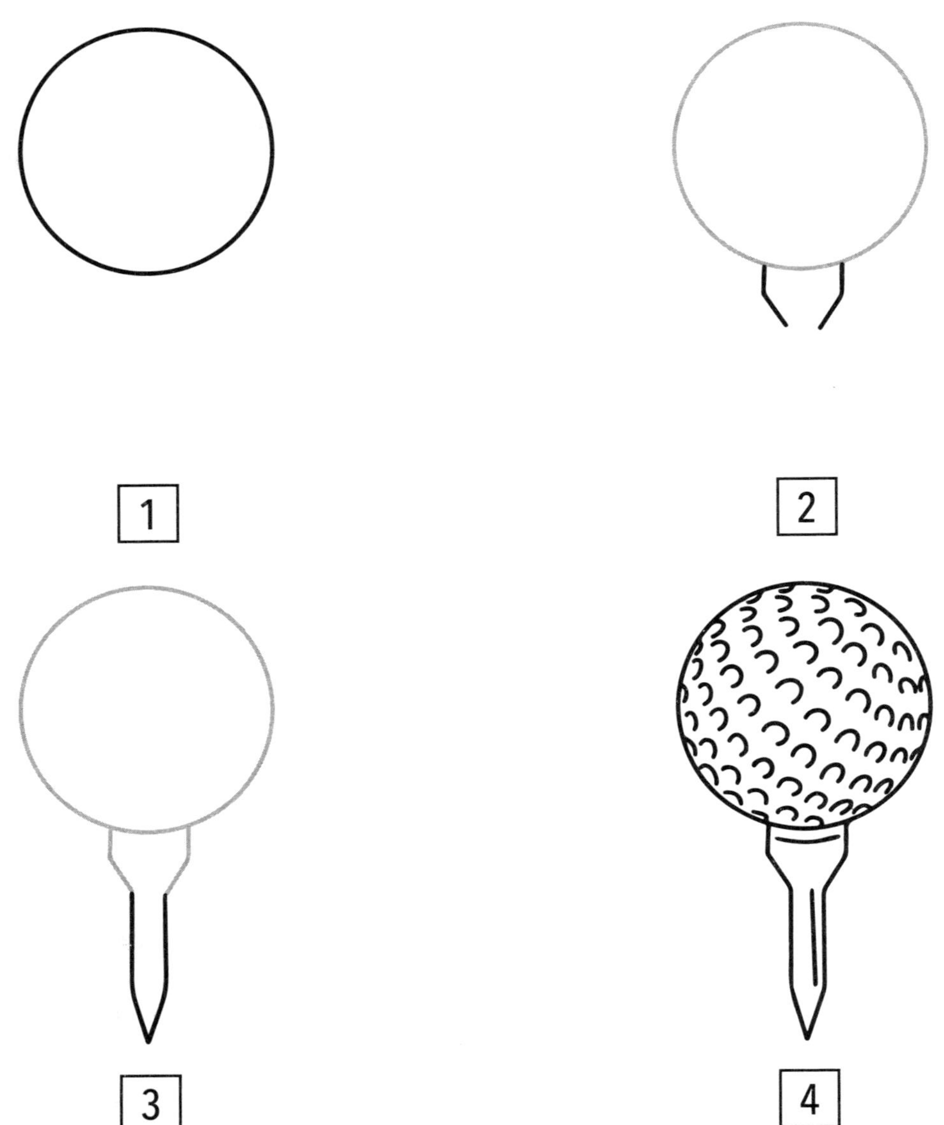

GOLF CULB

Early golf clubs had wooden shafts, but by the 1600s,
blacksmiths began forging metal heads for special clubs.

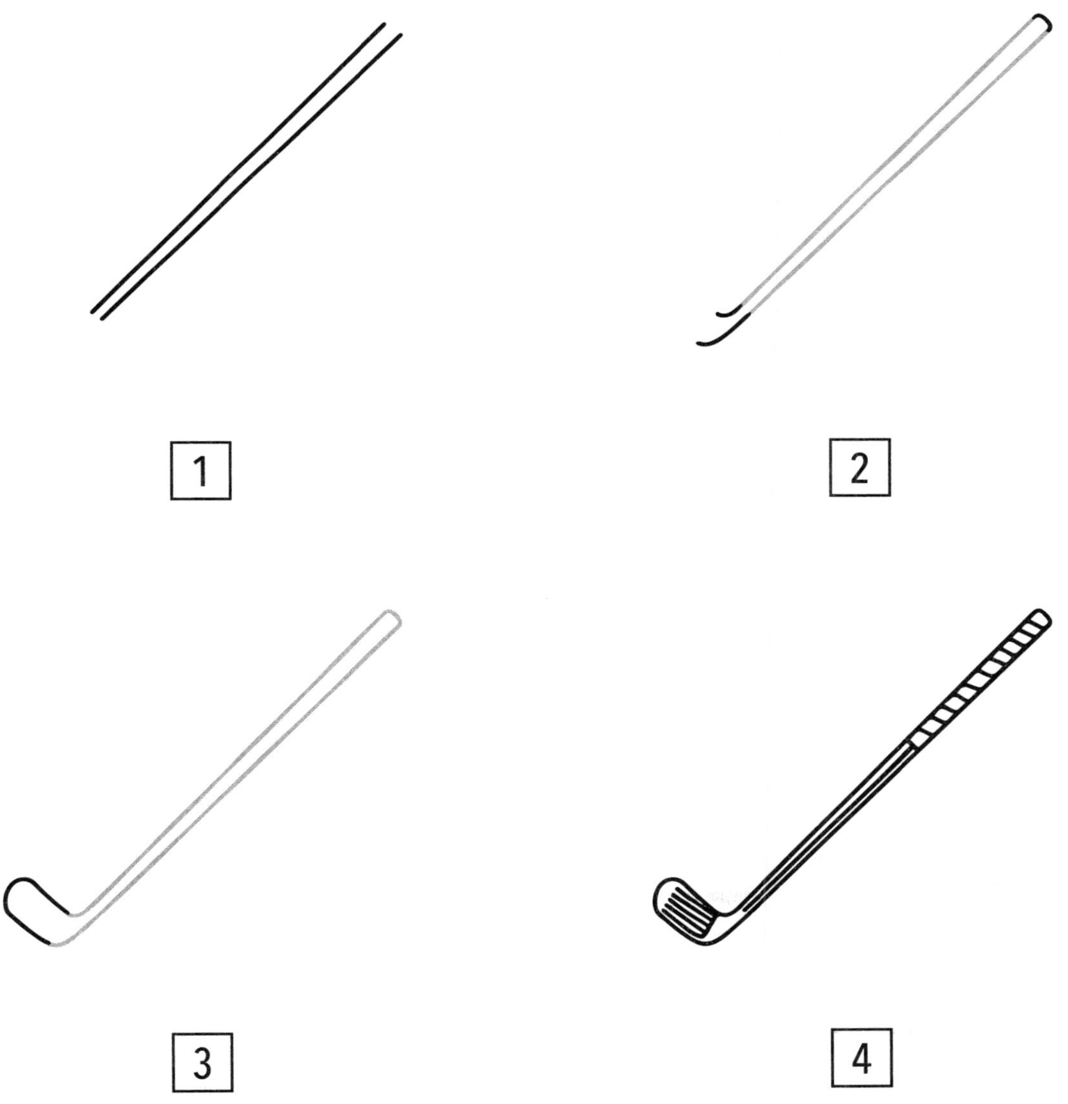

GOLF BAG

In the 1500s in Scotland, golfers started hiring helpers they called *cadets* to carry their heavy bags while playing. Today, they are called *caddies*.

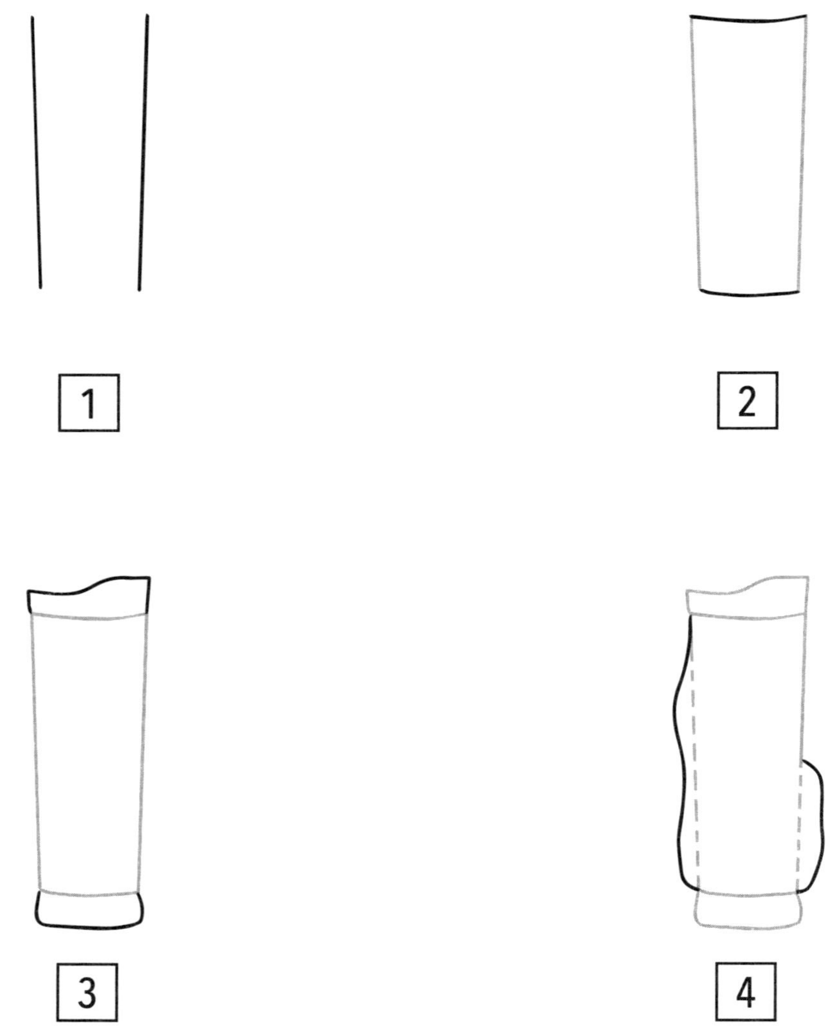

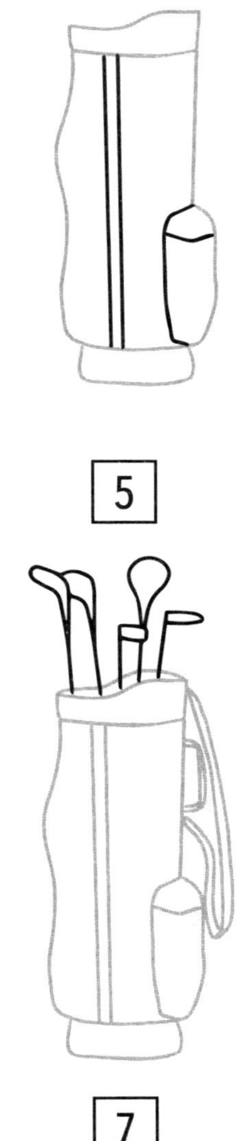

5

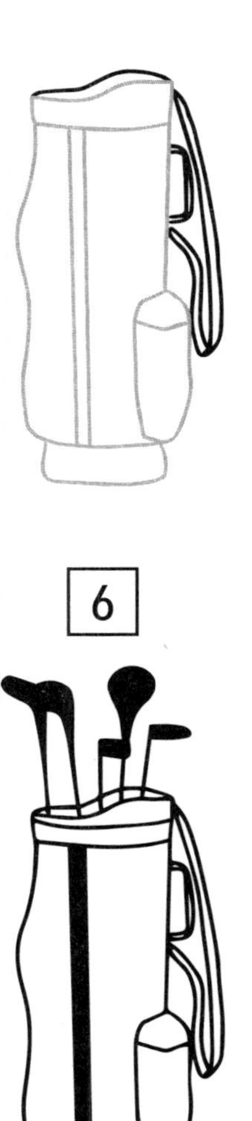

6

7

8

DIVING BOARD

Elite divers can spin through four and a half flips off a
10-meter platform before slicing into the water.

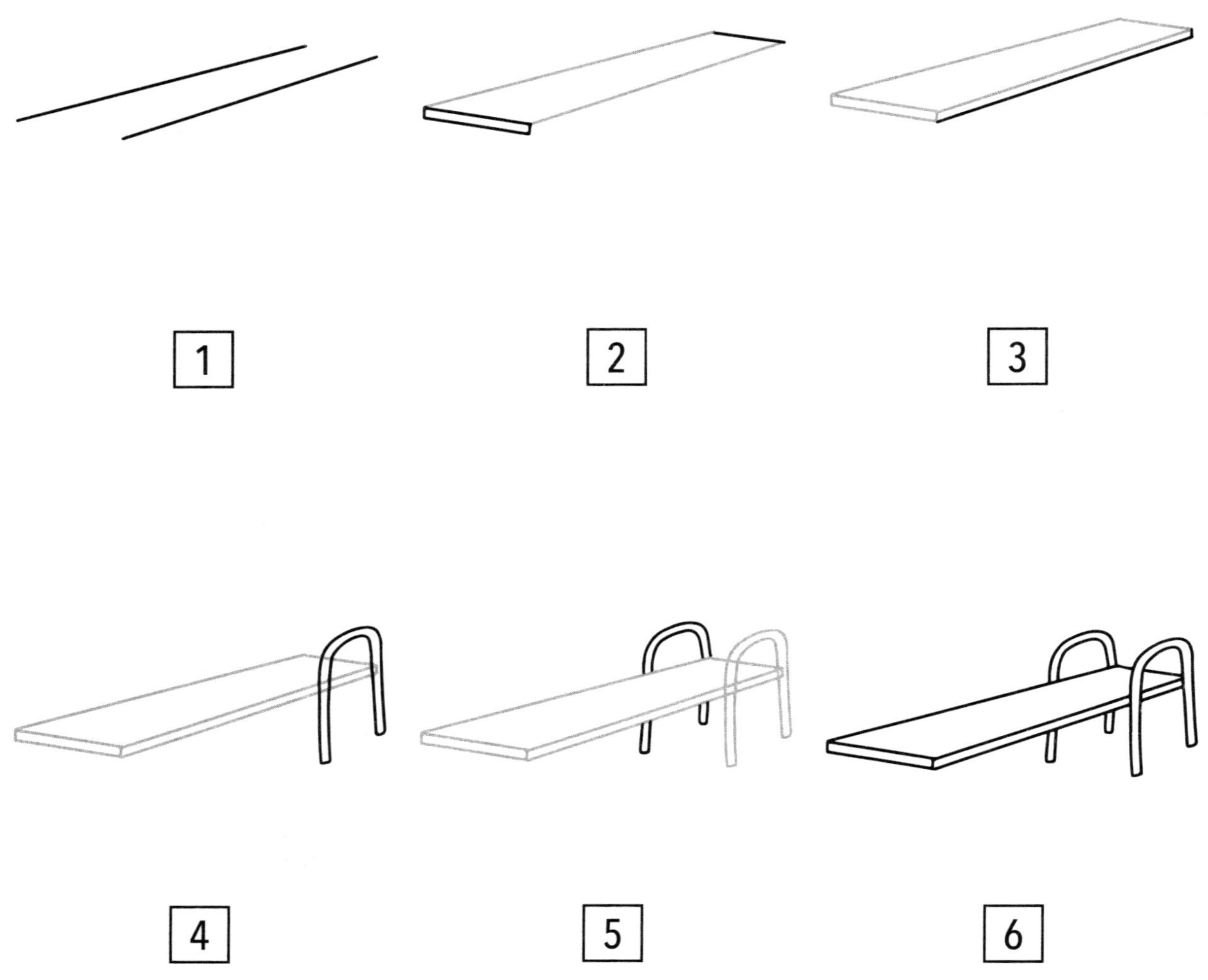

SWIM GOGGLES

The first swim goggles were made from tortoise shells!

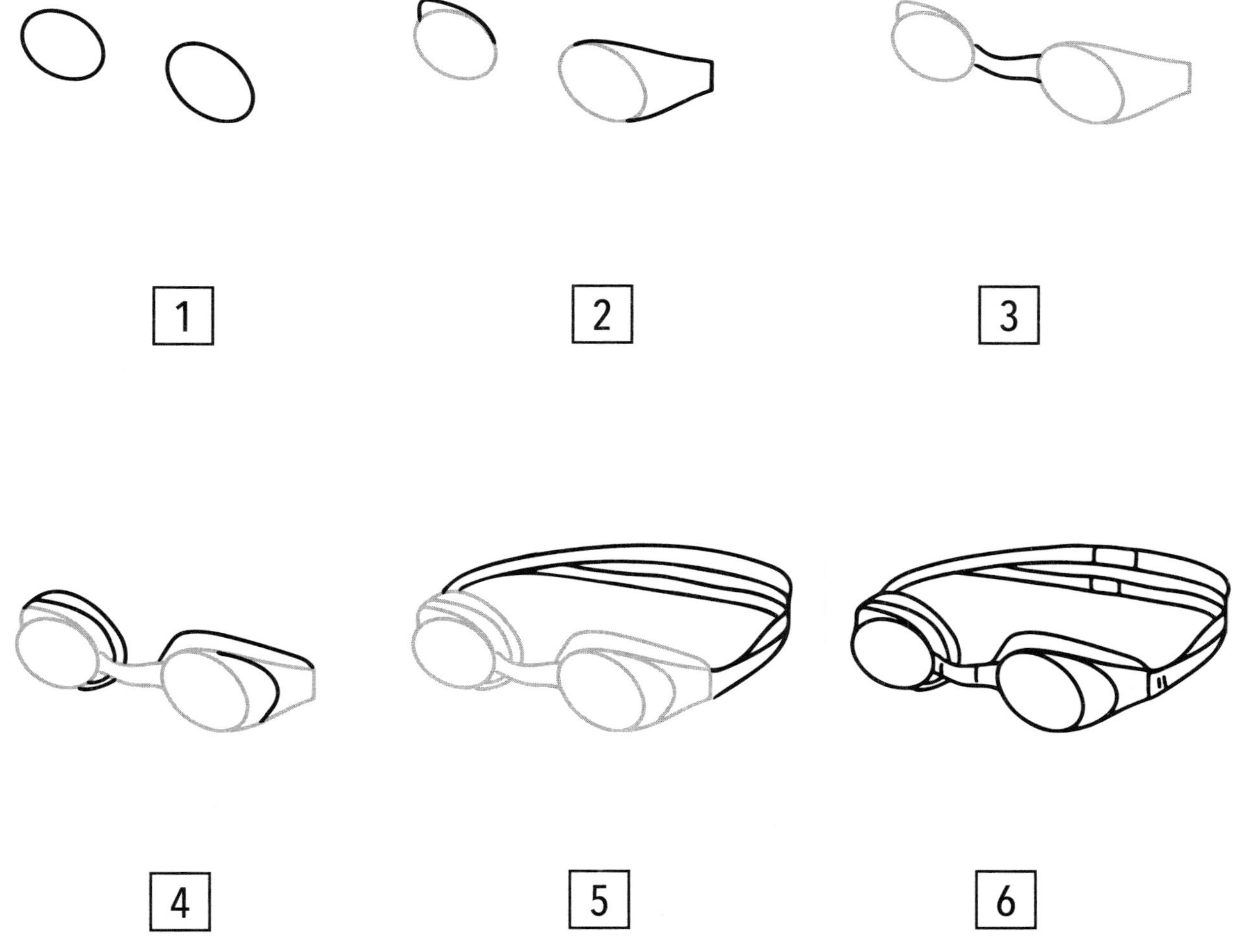

BOW AND ARROW

Archery dates back over 10,000 years. Ancient hunters used bows long before they were used in sports.

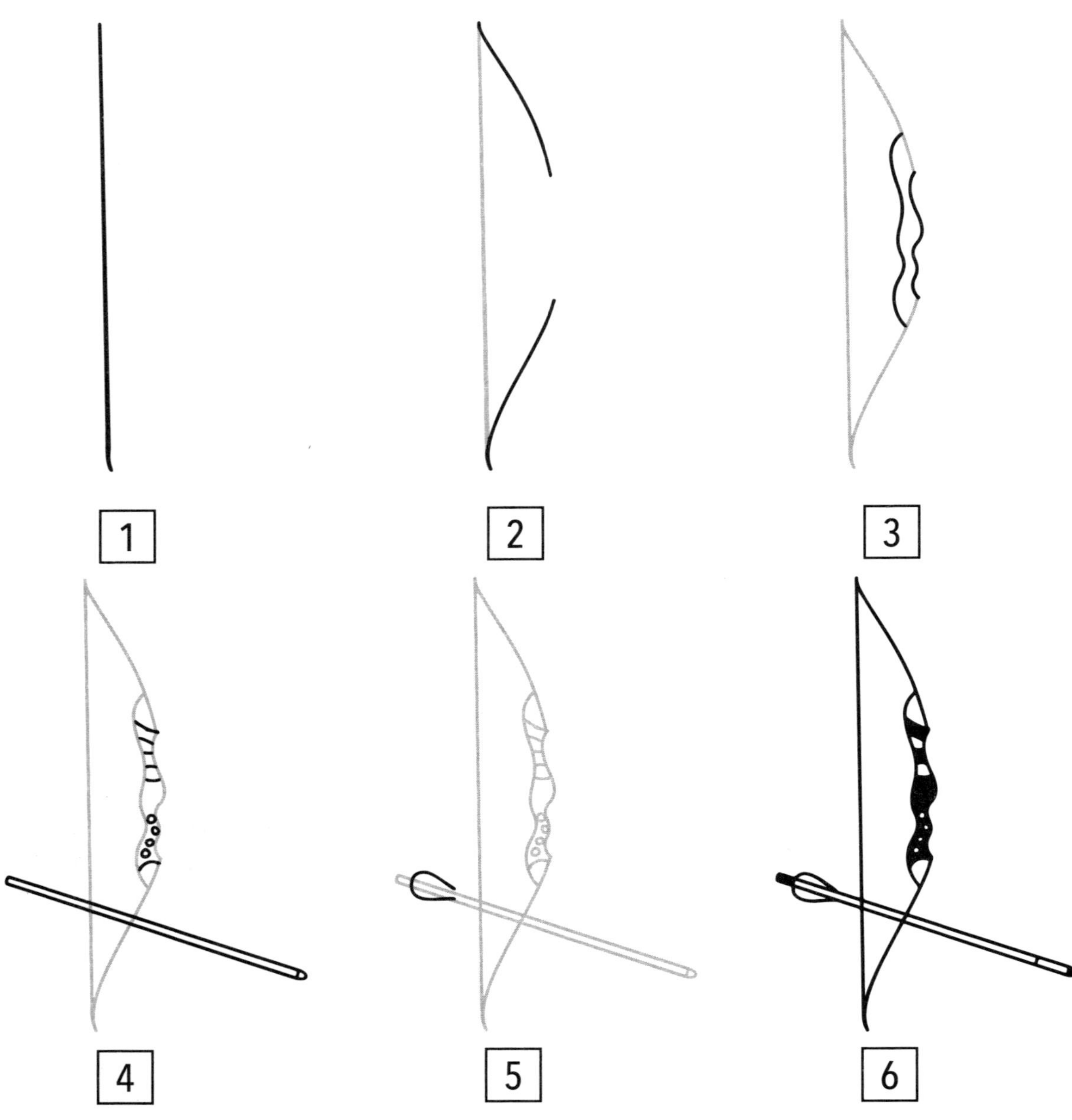

ARCHERY TARGET

Archery targets use five colors—white, black, blue, red, and gold—for the bullseye, the highest score.

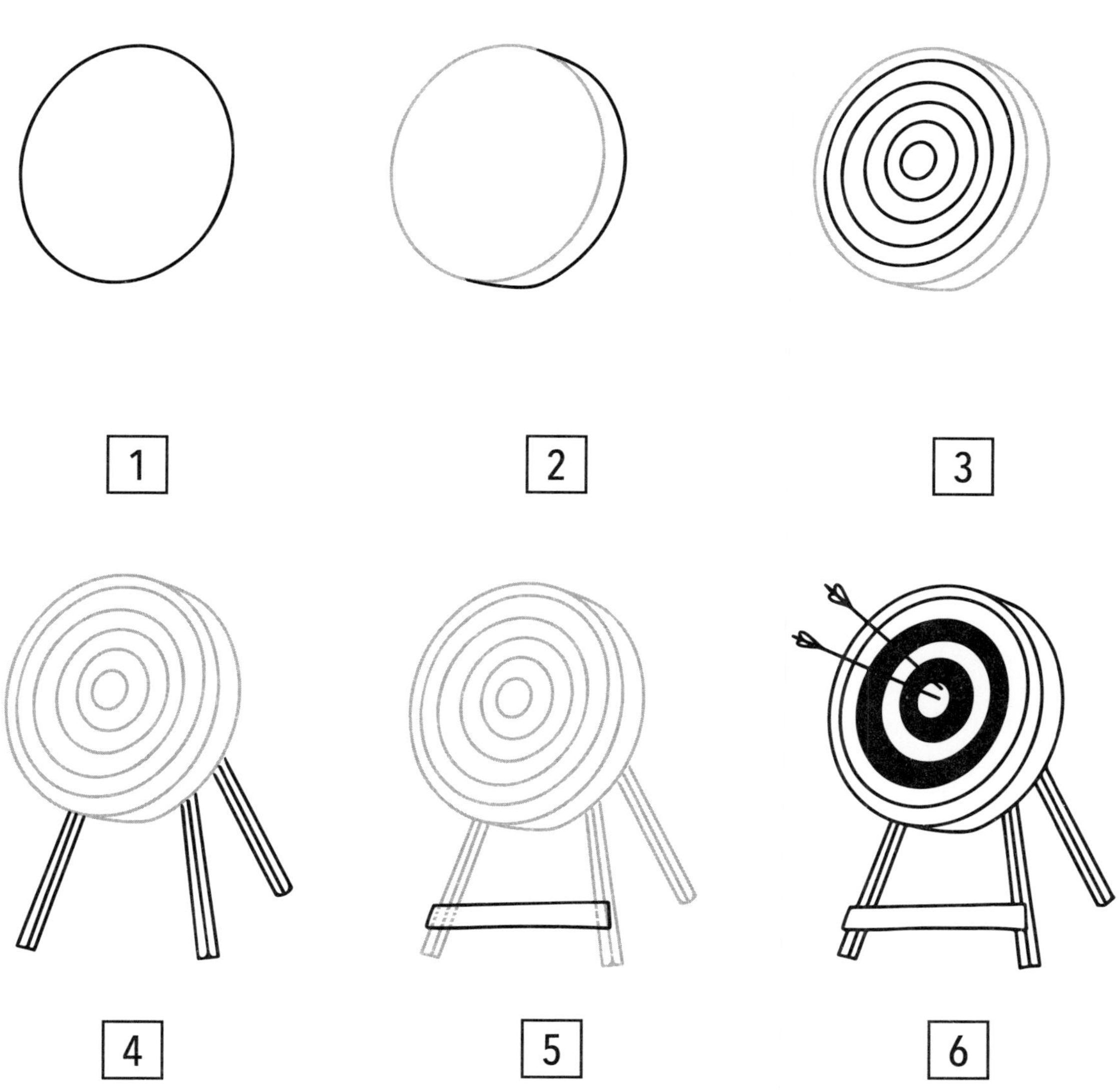

BALANCE BEAM

A balance beam is only four inches wide—about the same as a smartphone screen.

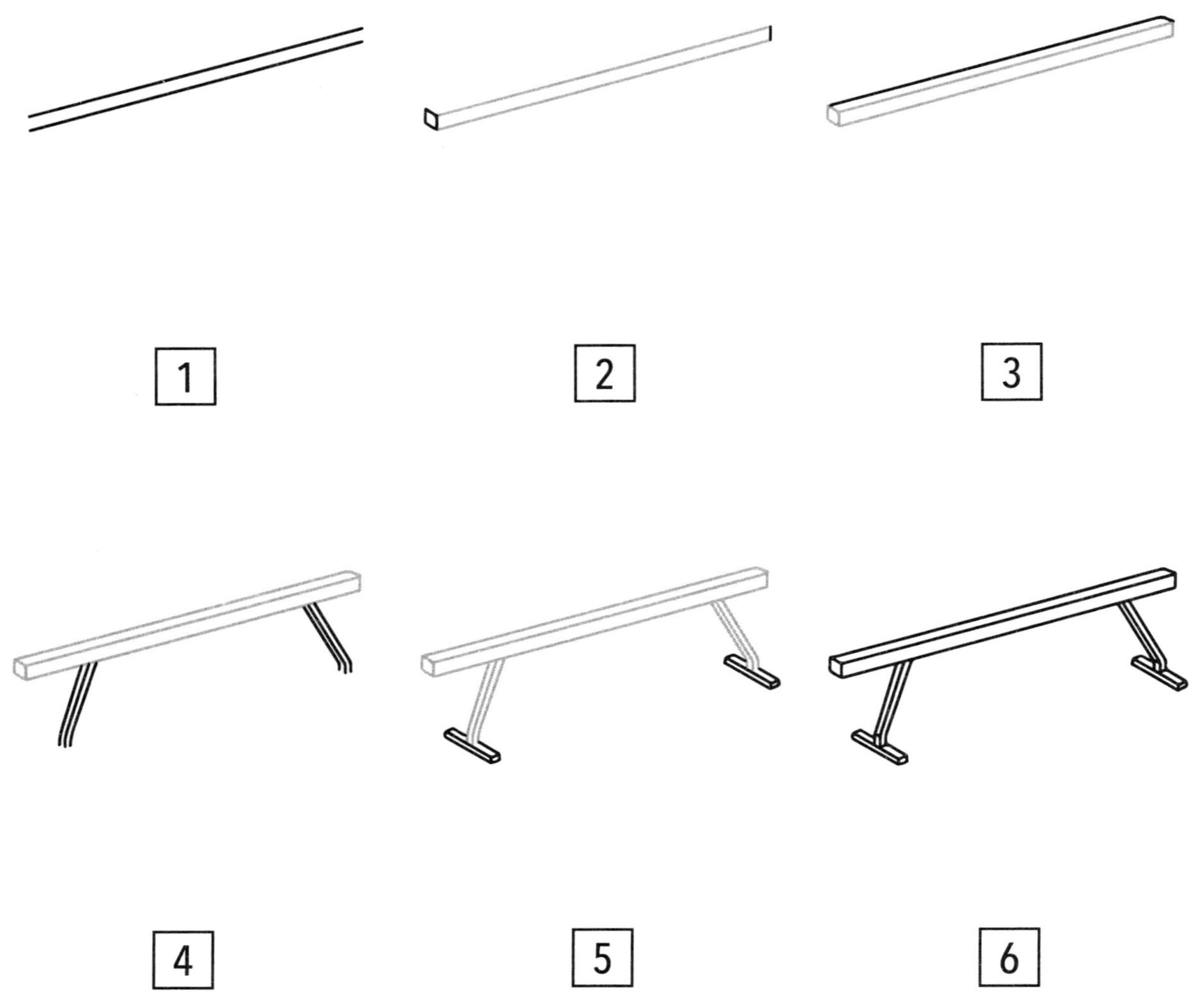

UNEVEN BARS

Gymnasts switch between the high and low bar using flips,
swings, and releases that take years to master.

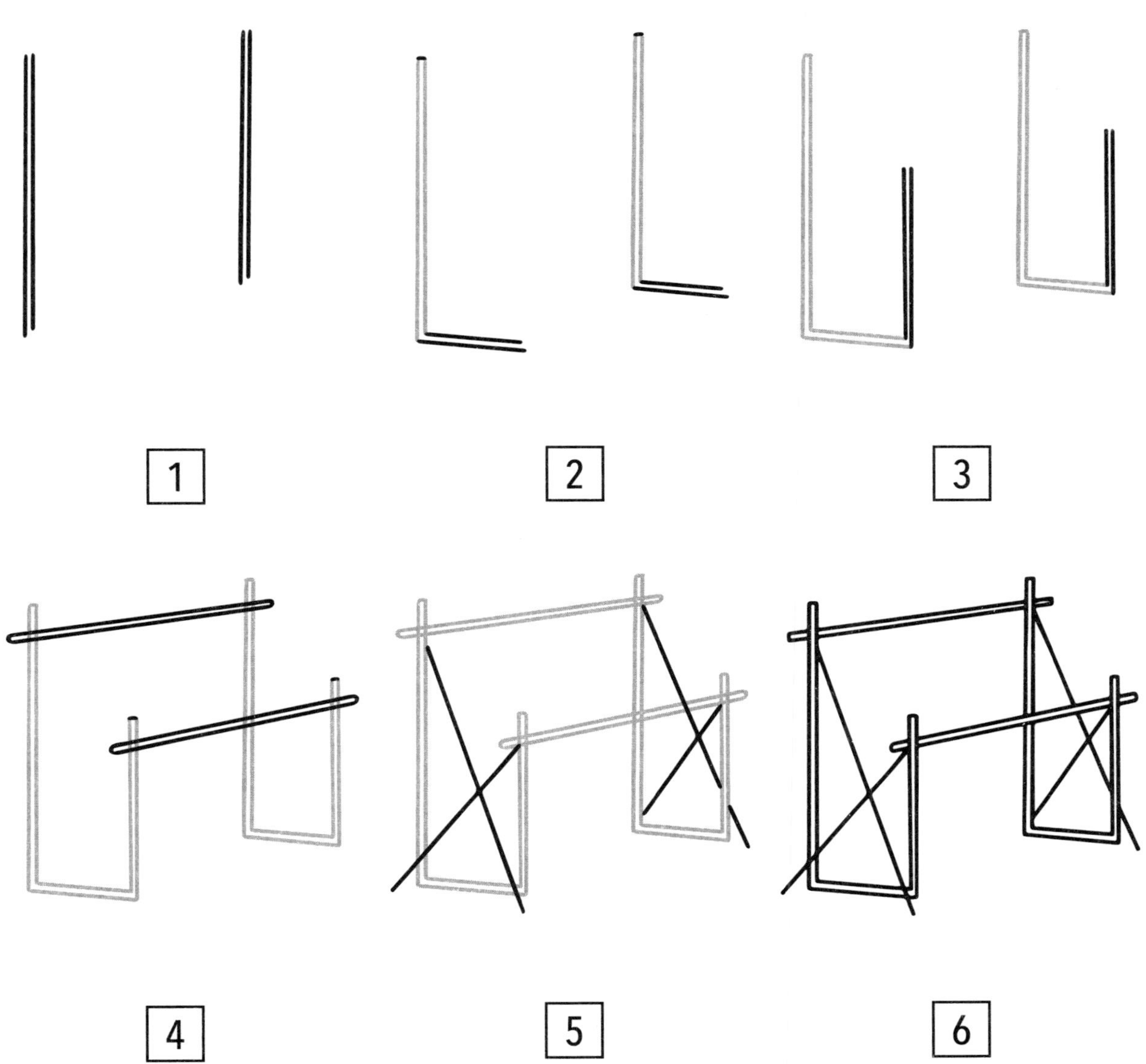

BASEBALL

A professional baseball has exactly 108 double stitches
and uses a mile of thread to make just one ball.

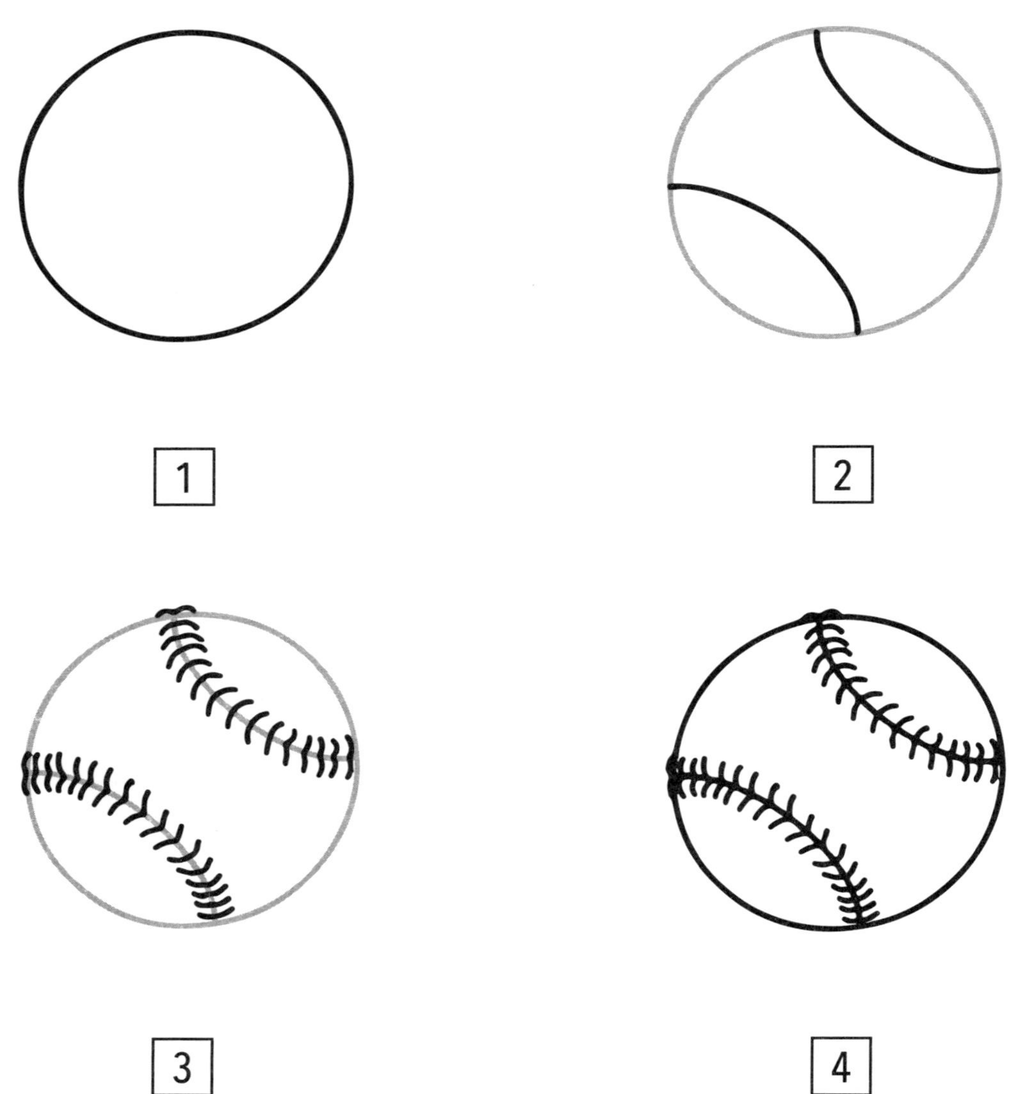

BASEBALL BAT

The crack of a wooden bat hitting a baseball can reach over 100 decibels—almost as loud as a chainsaw.

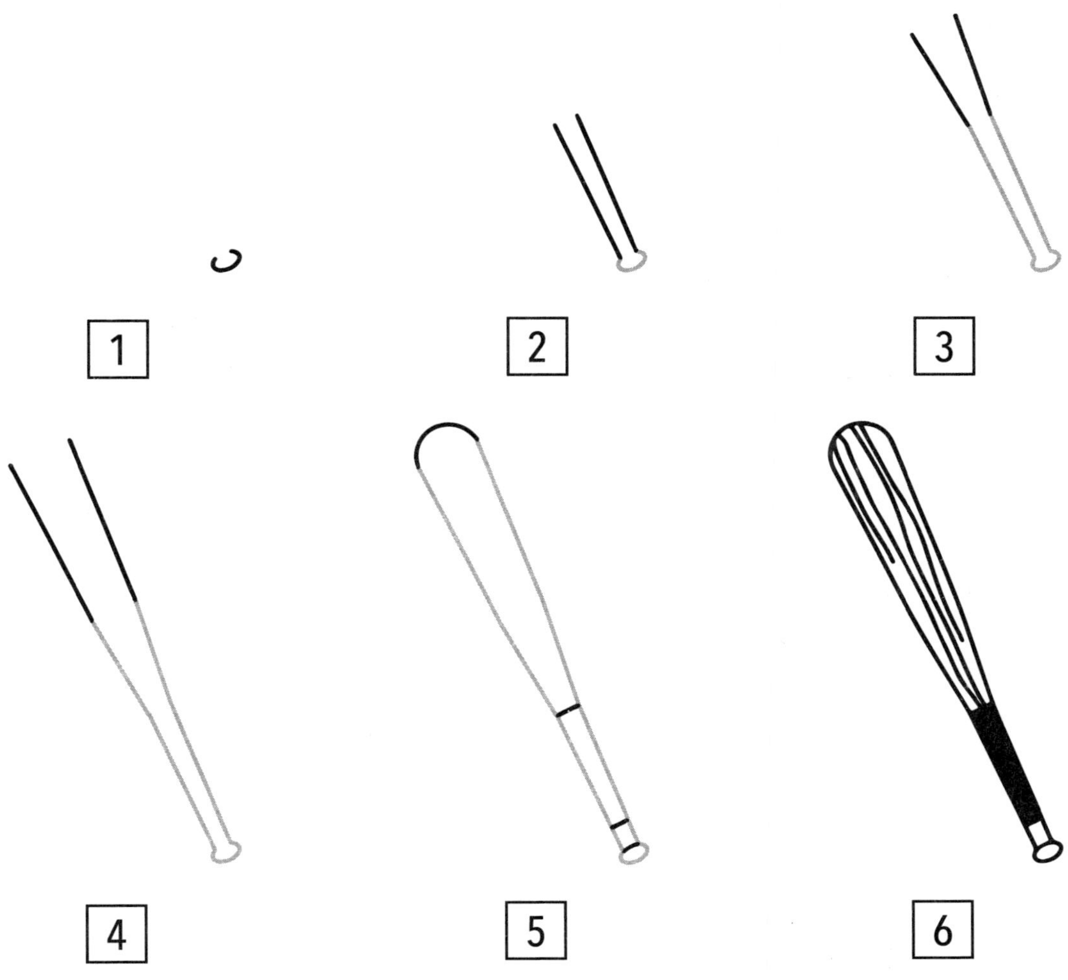

BASEBALL GLOVE

Baseball gloves were first worn in the 1870s, but players were teased because people thought using them meant they weren't tough enough.

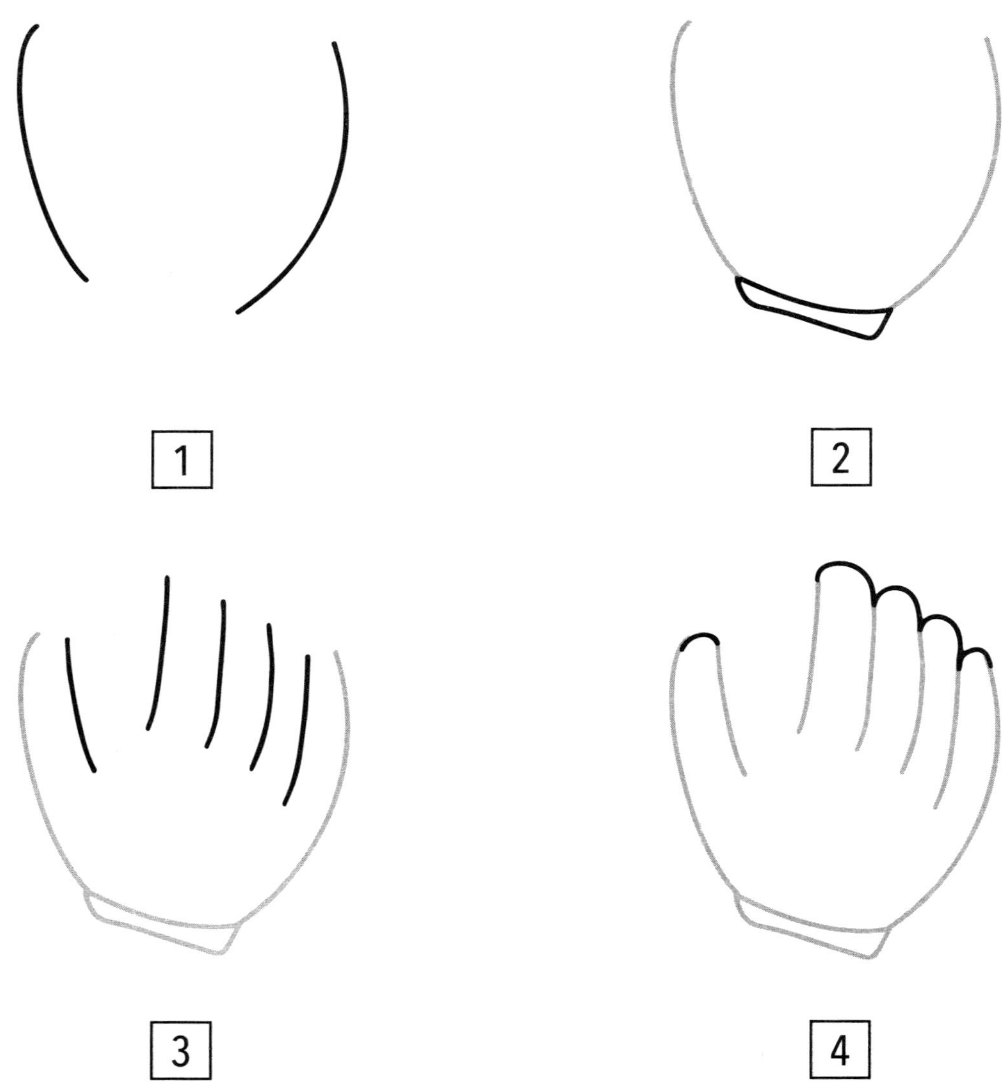

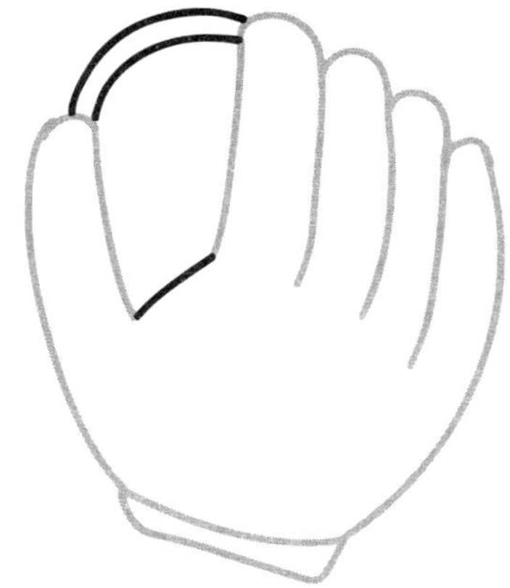

5

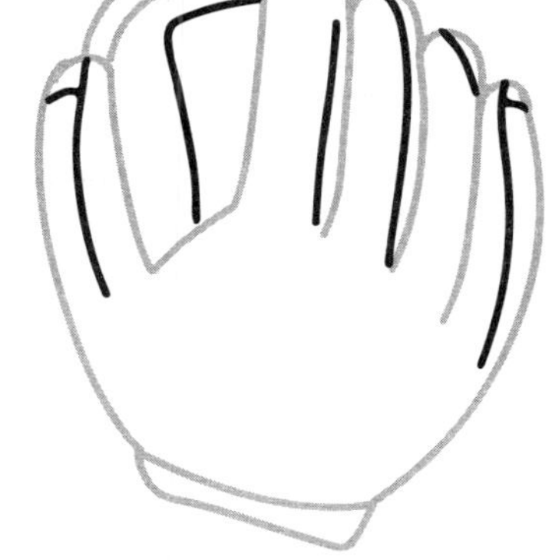

6

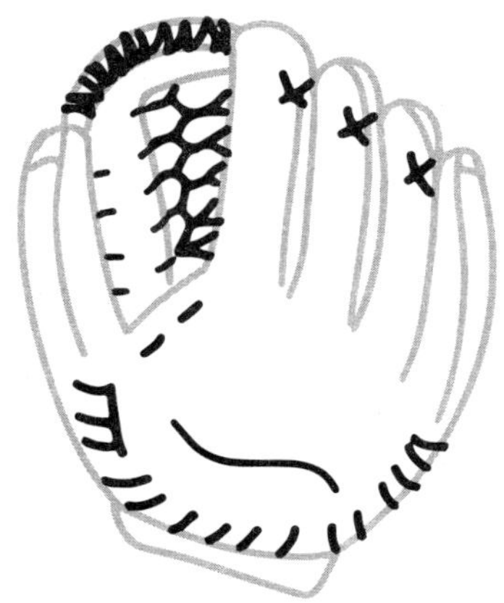

7

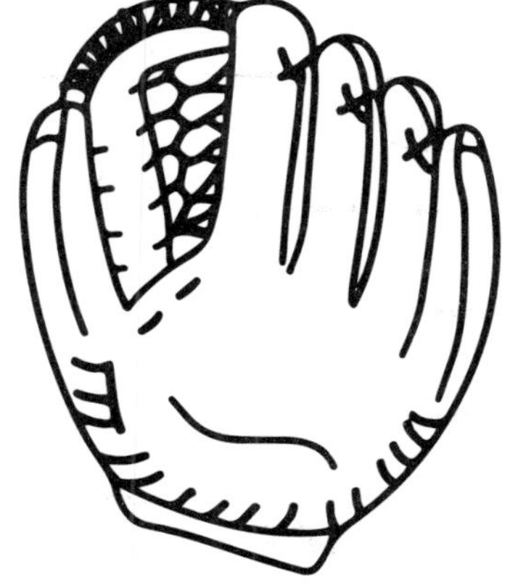

8

PICKLEBALL

Pickleball was named after the inventor's dog, Pickles, who loved chasing stray balls during backyard games.

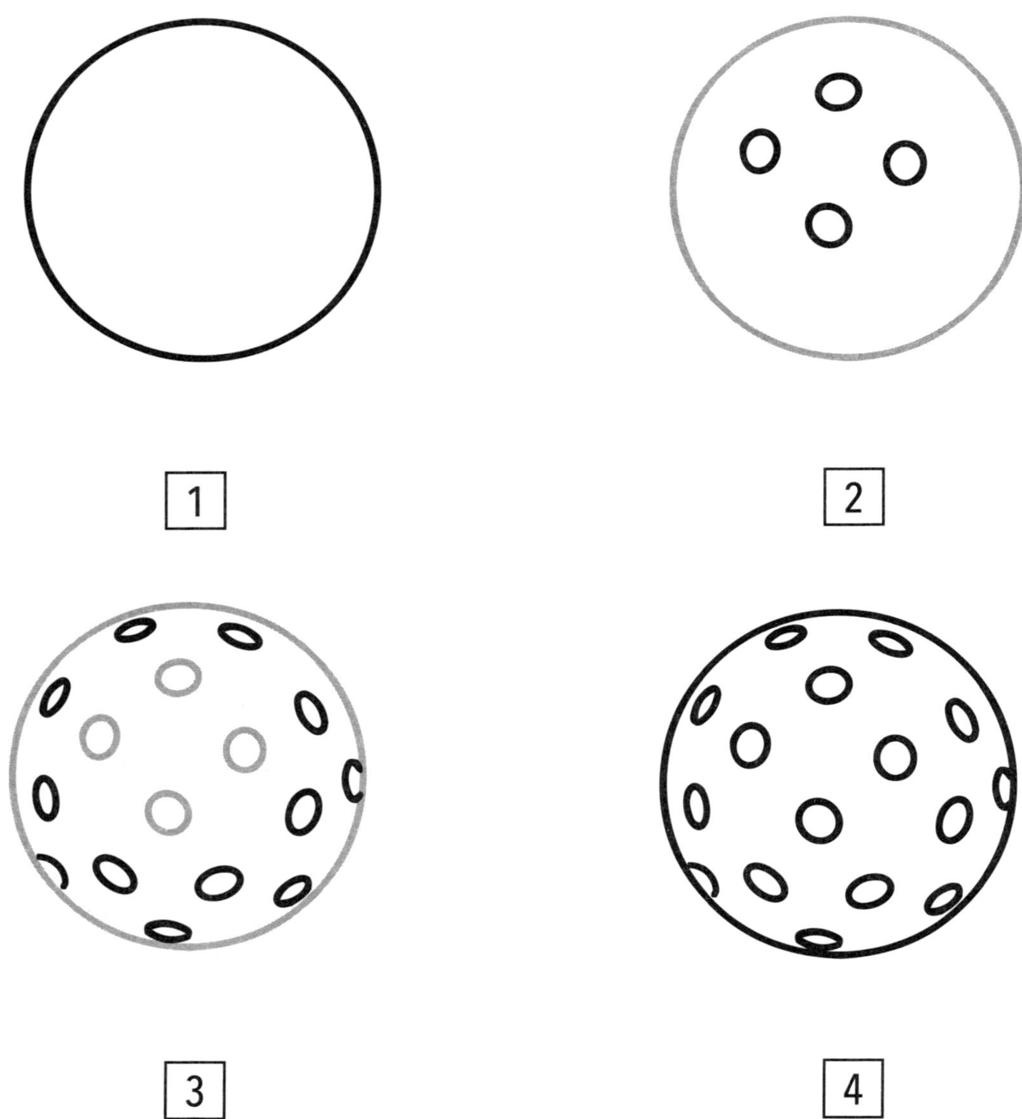

PICKLEBALL PADDLE

Pickleball is the fastest-growing sport in the United States, with millions of new players picking up a paddle every year.

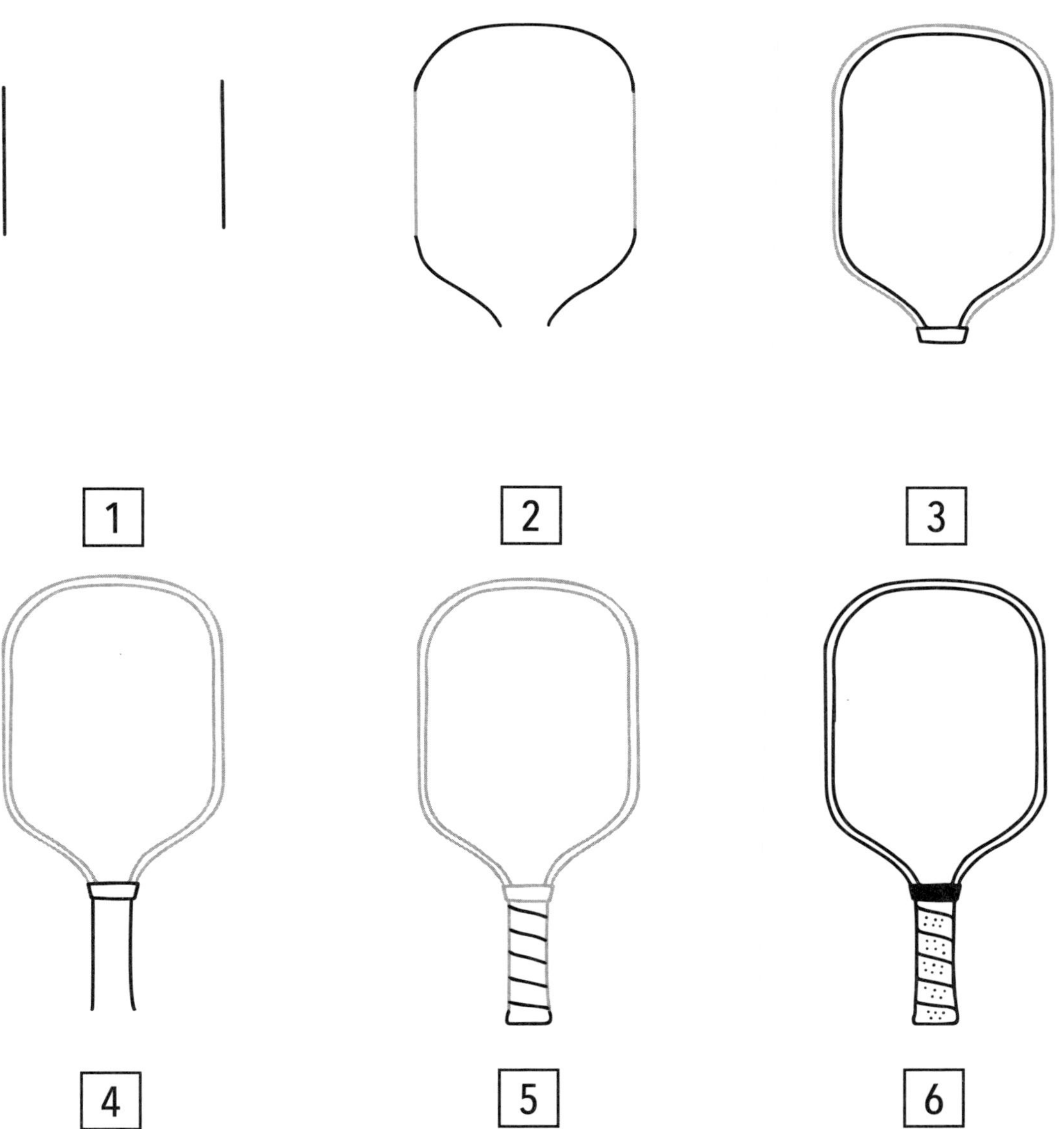

TENNIS BALL

Tennis balls used to be white or black. Now they're neon yellow so players and fans can see them better on television.

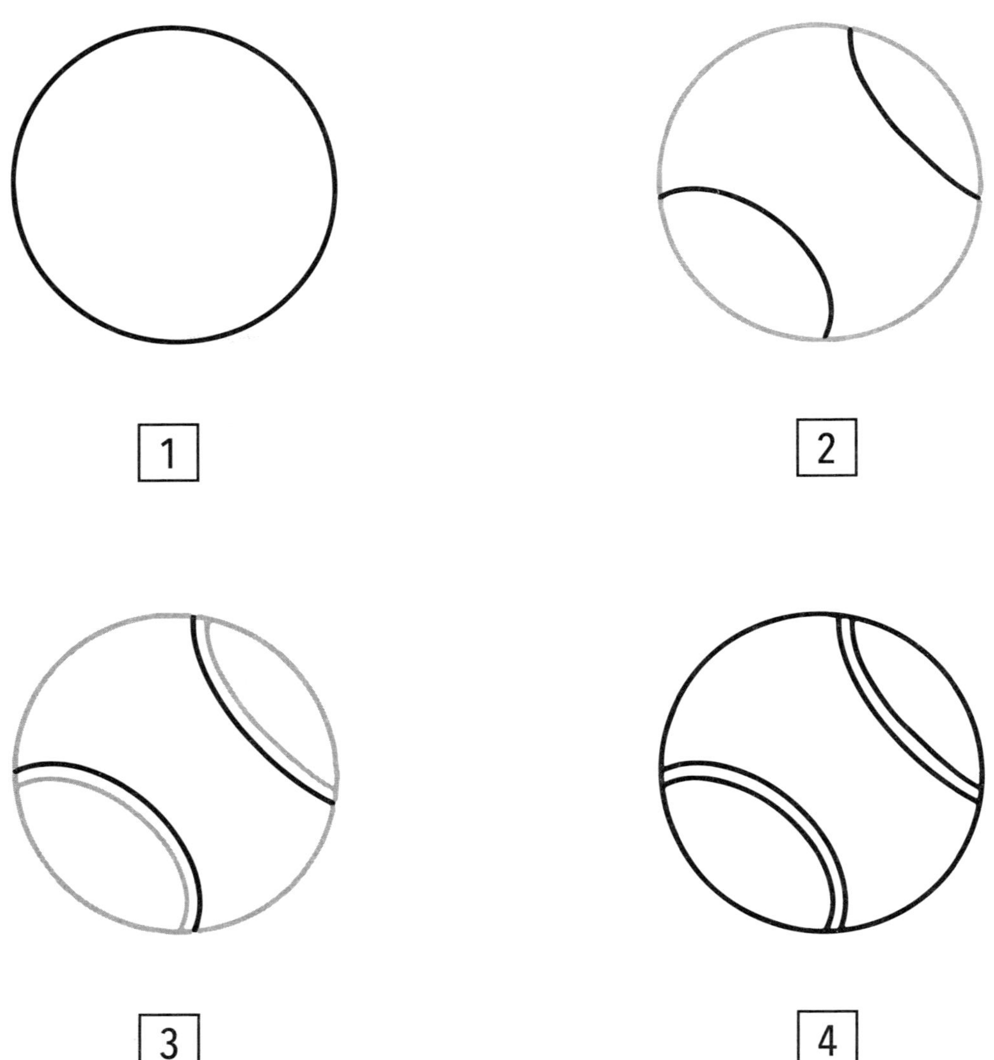

TENNIS RACKET

Early tennis rackets were made of wood and strung with sheep intestines.
Today's are made from graphite or carbon fiber.

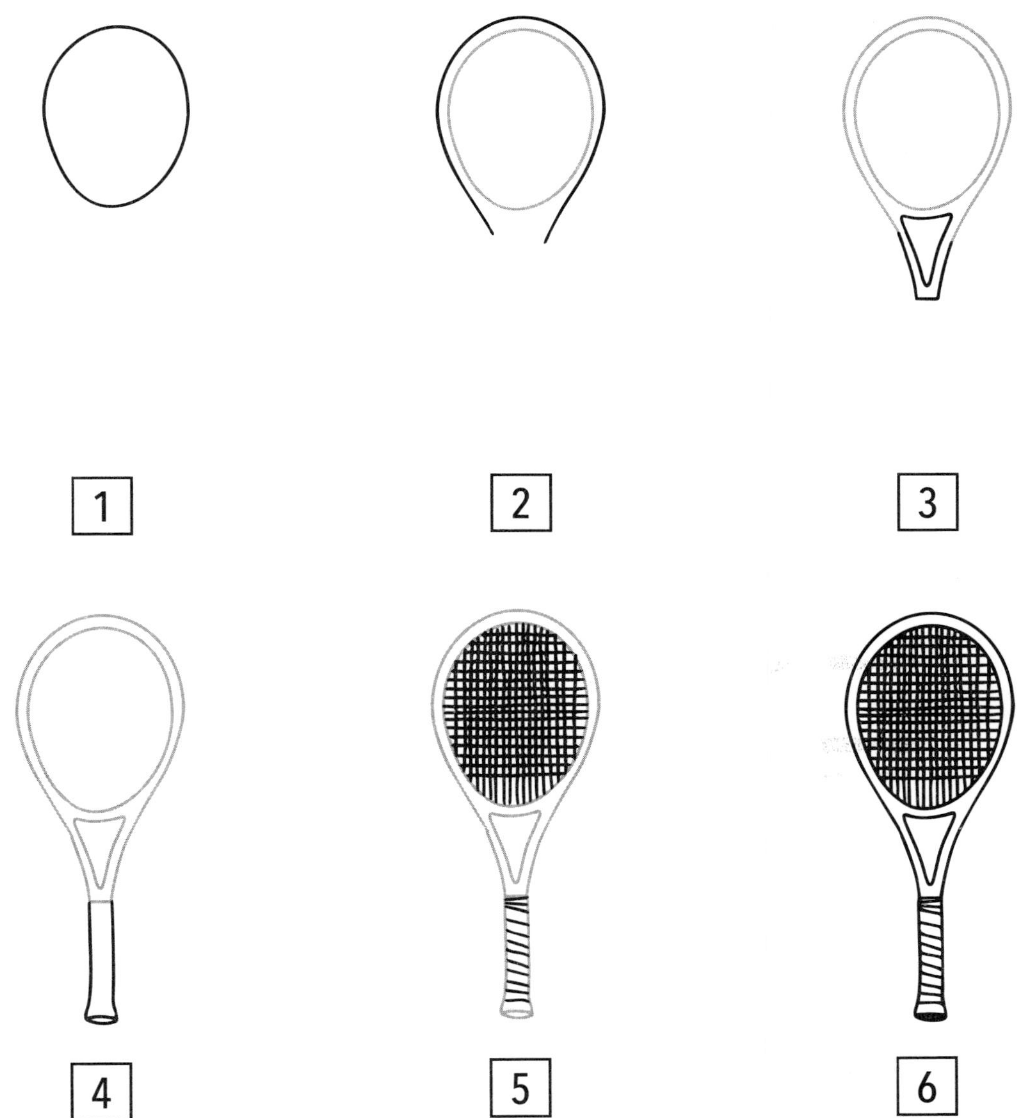

BALLET SHOES

Ballet dancers go through dozens of shoes every season.
Some professionals wear out a pair after just one performance!

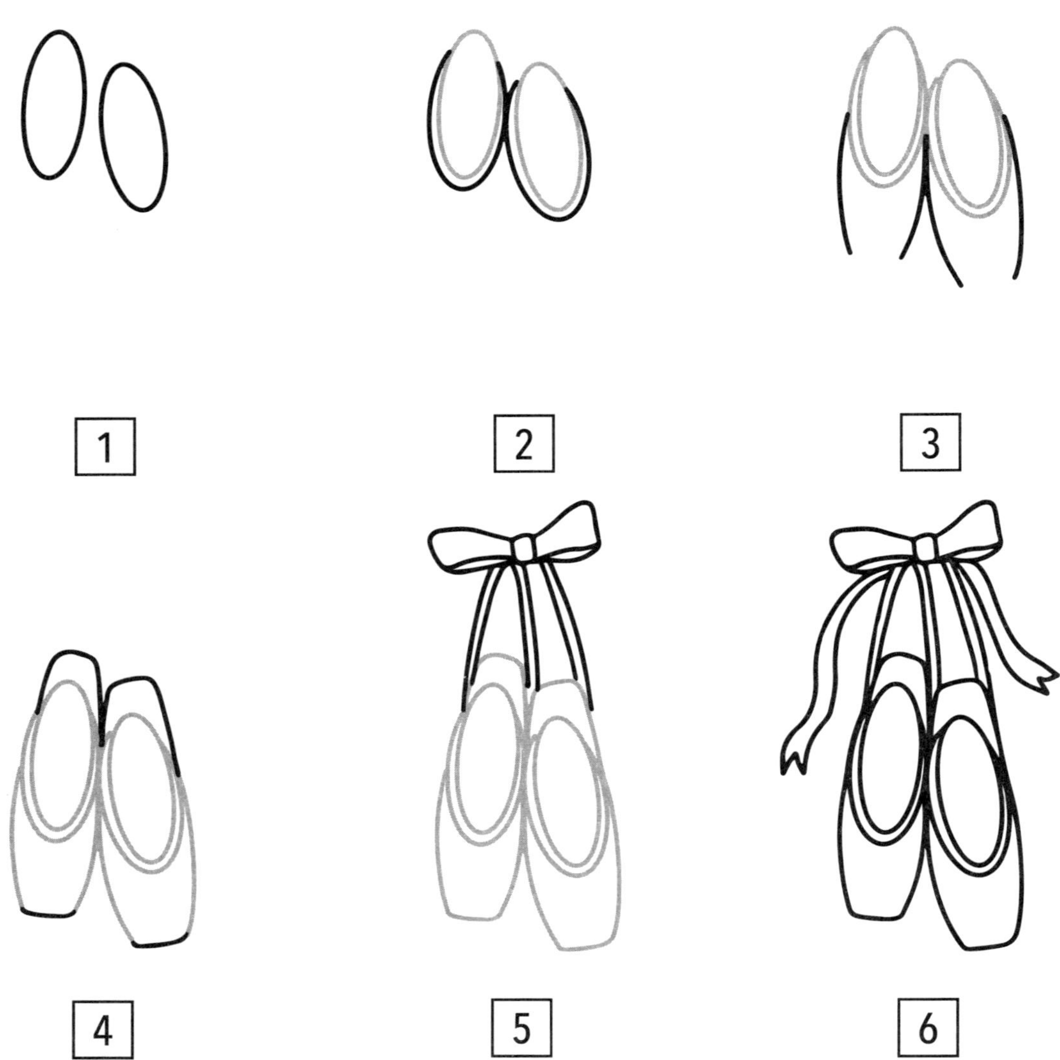

POM-POMS

Pom-poms were once made of paper. Now they're plastic and come in all varieties—metallic, glitter, and even holographic.

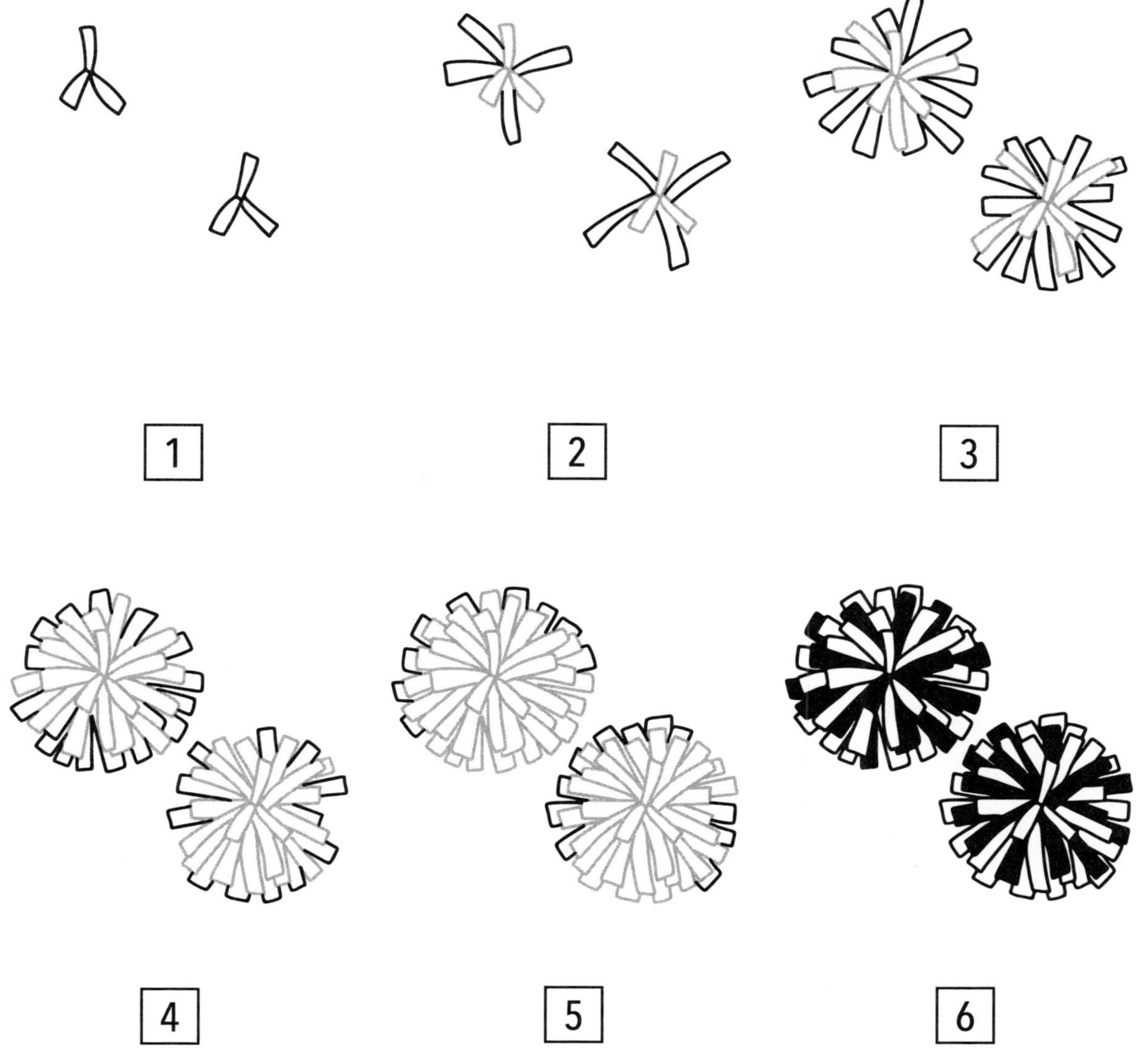

SKATEBOARD

The first skateboards were made from wooden boxes with roller skate wheels screwed to the bottom.

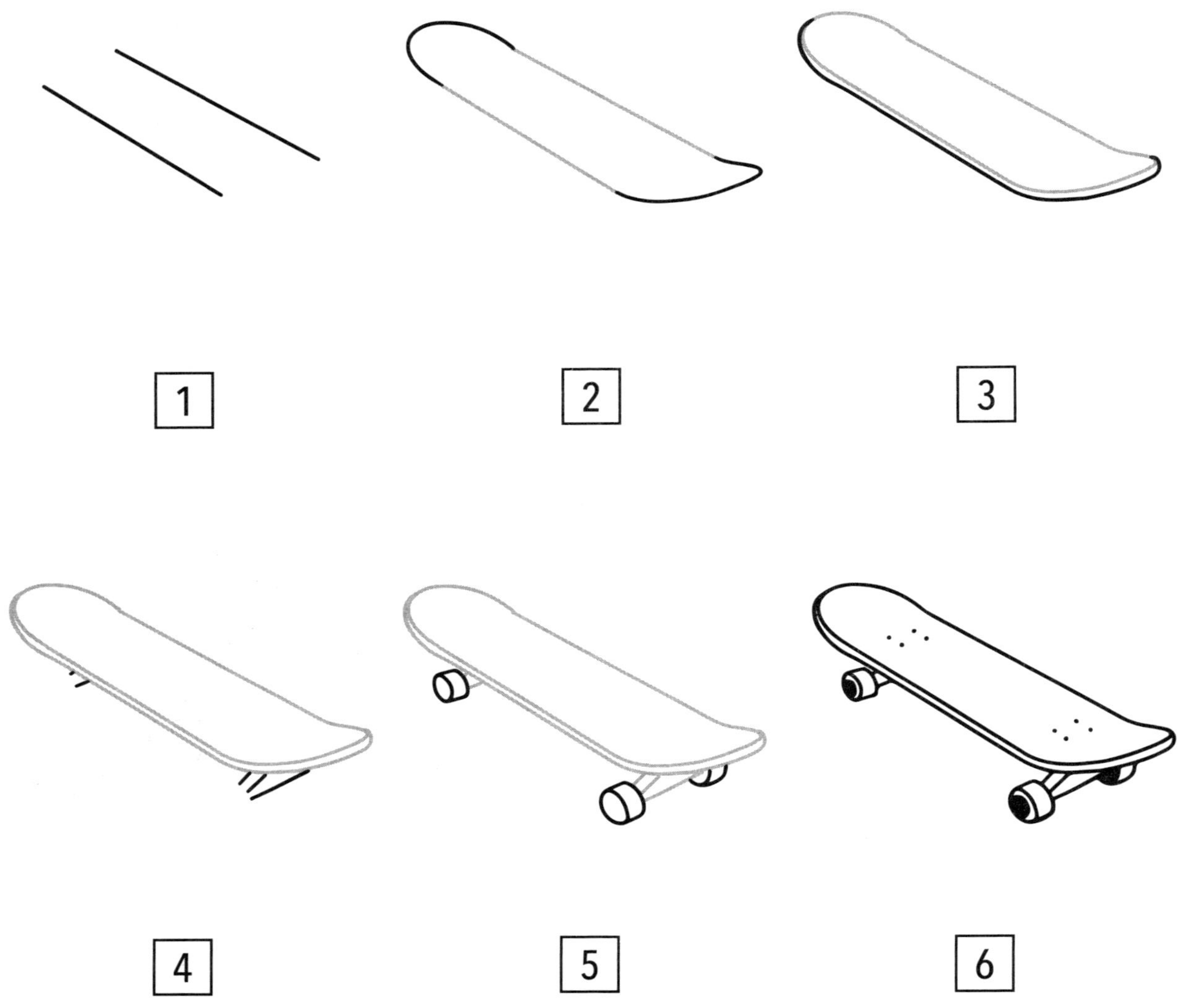

SCOOTER

Scooter tricks like tailwhips and barspins are now part of pro competitions—some riders can even do flips!

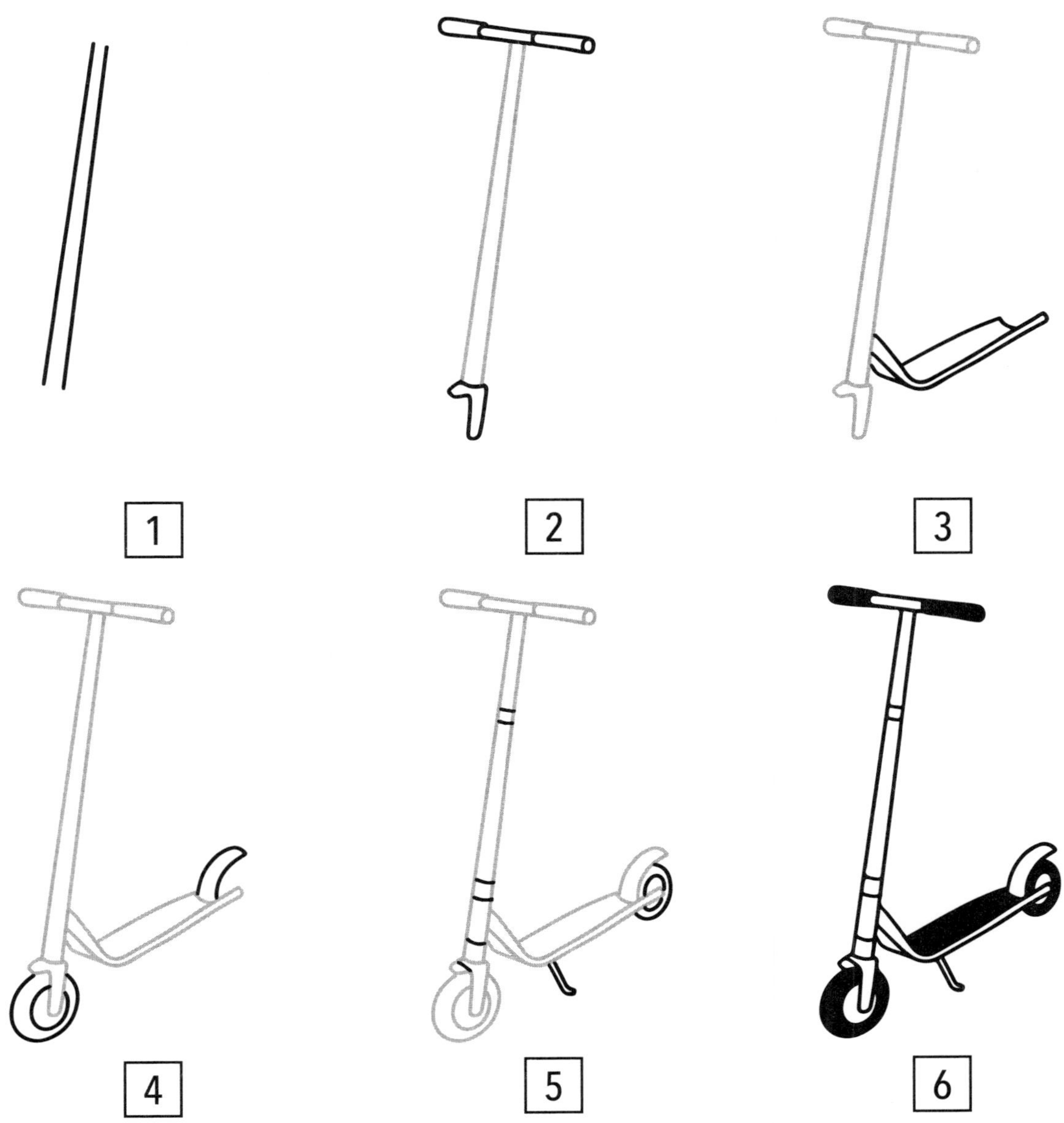

BICYCLE

The longest tandem bicycle ever built could seat 35 people and was over 65 feet long!

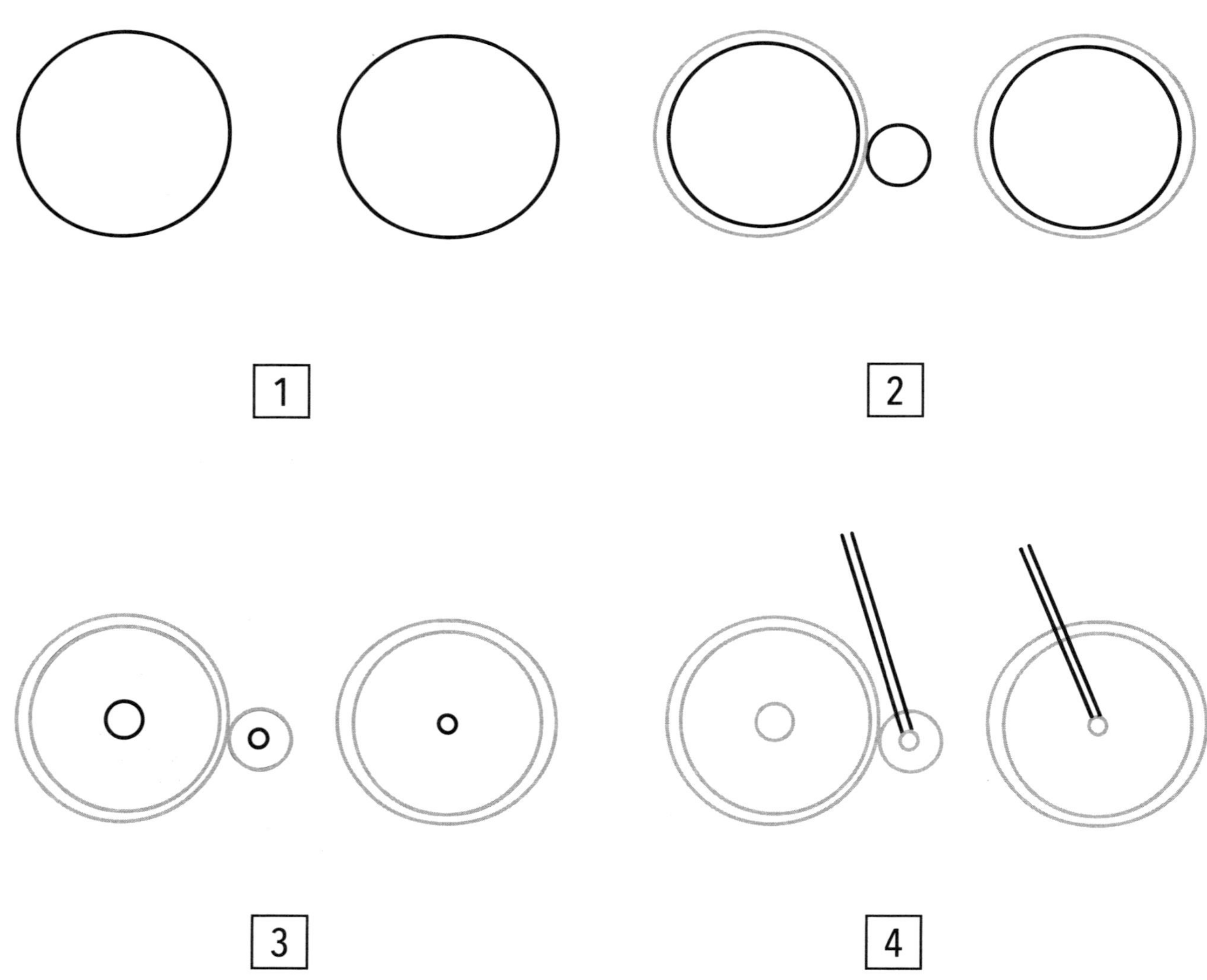

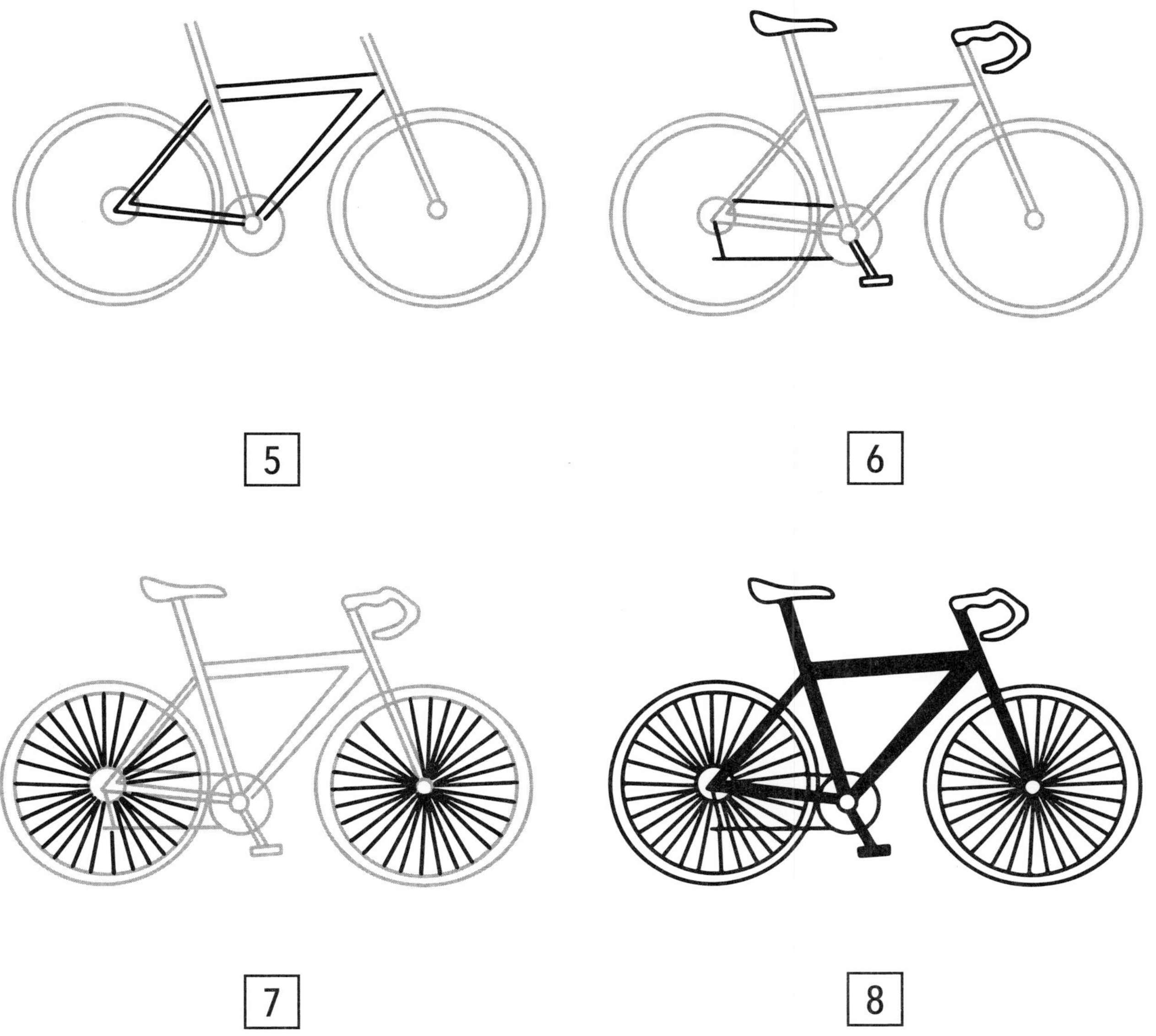

5

6

7

8

HELMET

Before a new helmet design hits store shelves, it's smashed, dropped, and crushed in lab tests to make sure it can protect your noggin in a real crash.

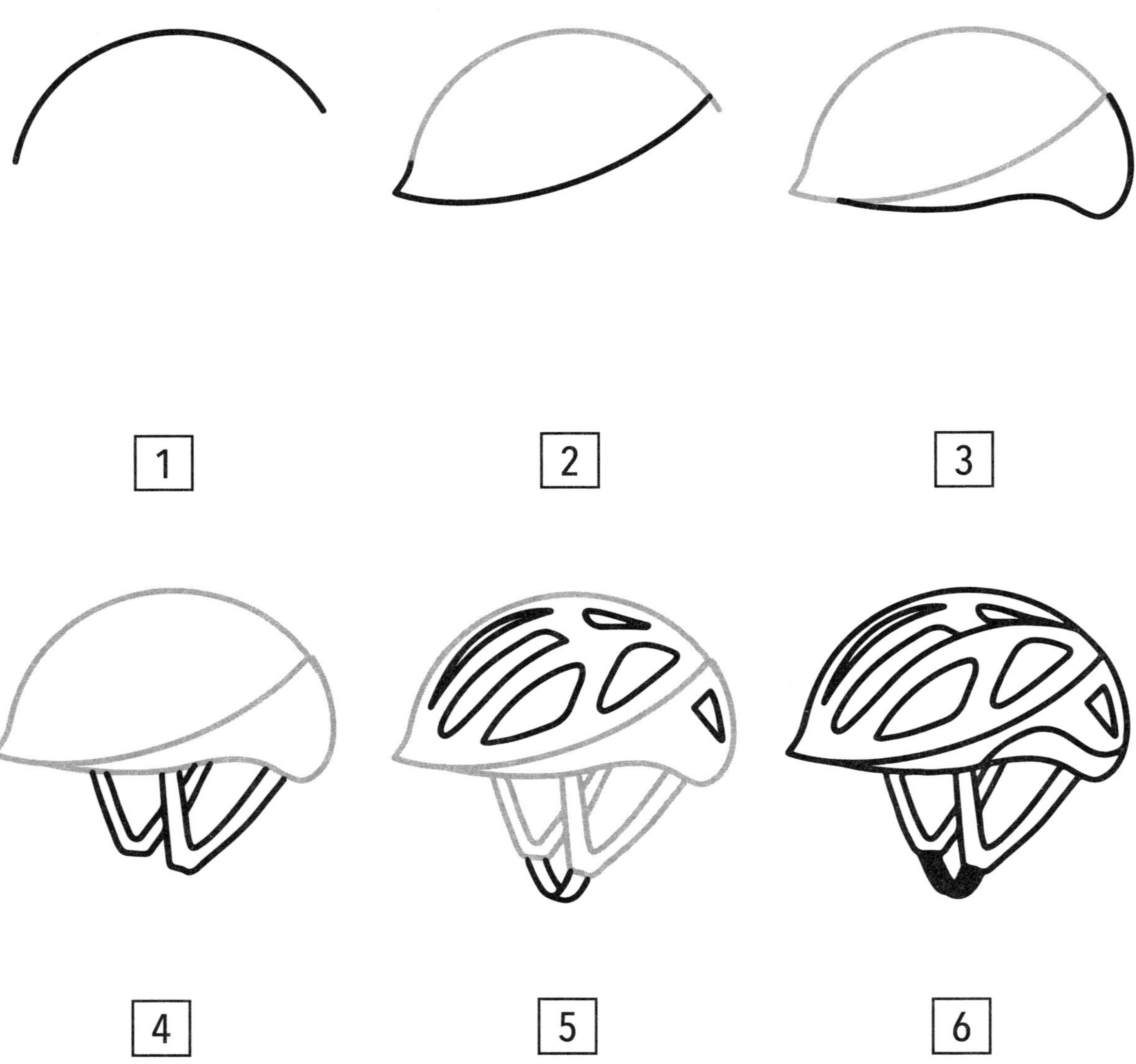

KNEEPADS

Kneepads use foam or gel padding to absorb impact and spread out force, protecting your joints from injury during falls.

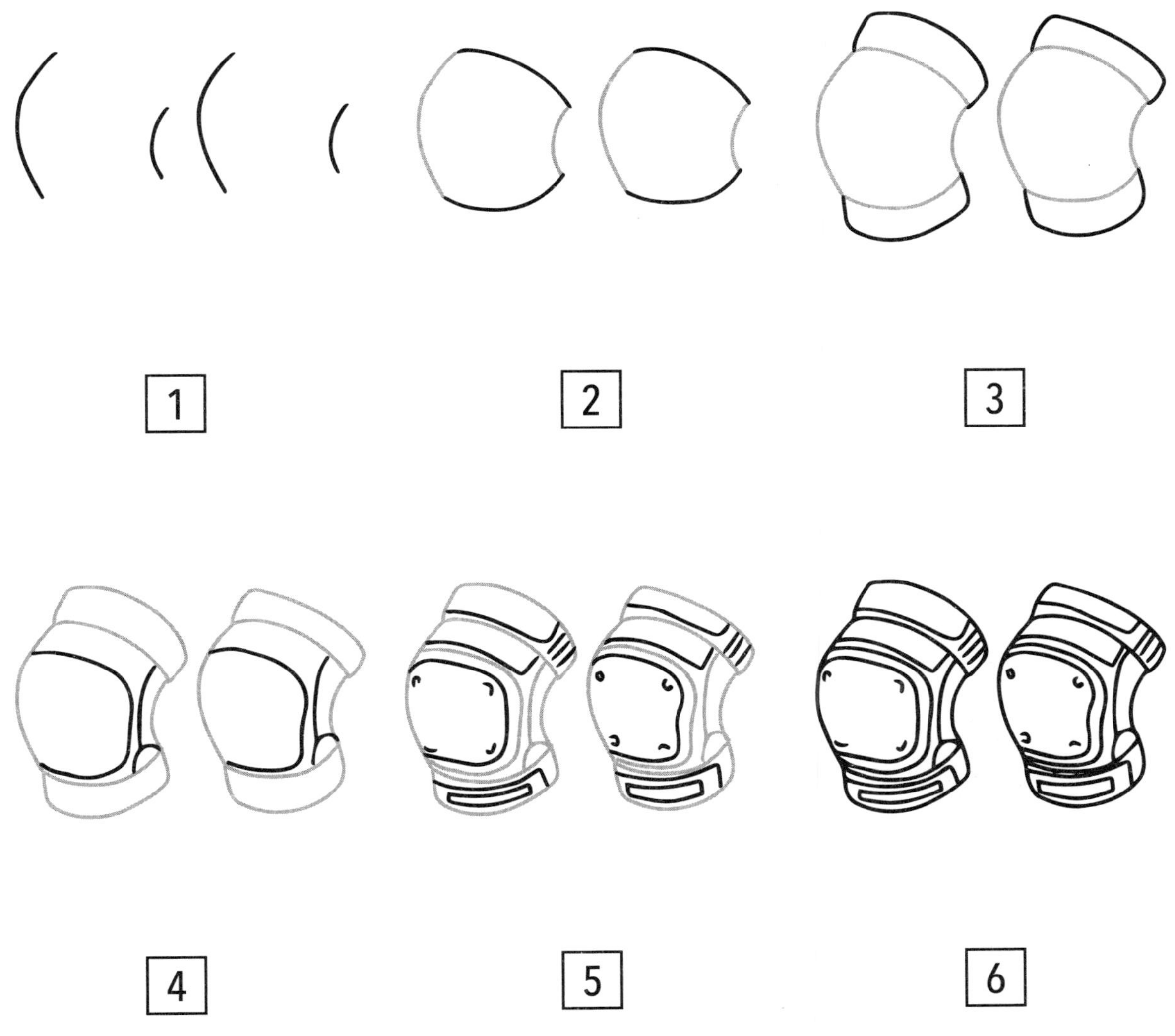

LEOTARD

The leotard is named after Jules Léotard, a French acrobat
who made the outfit popular in the 1800s.

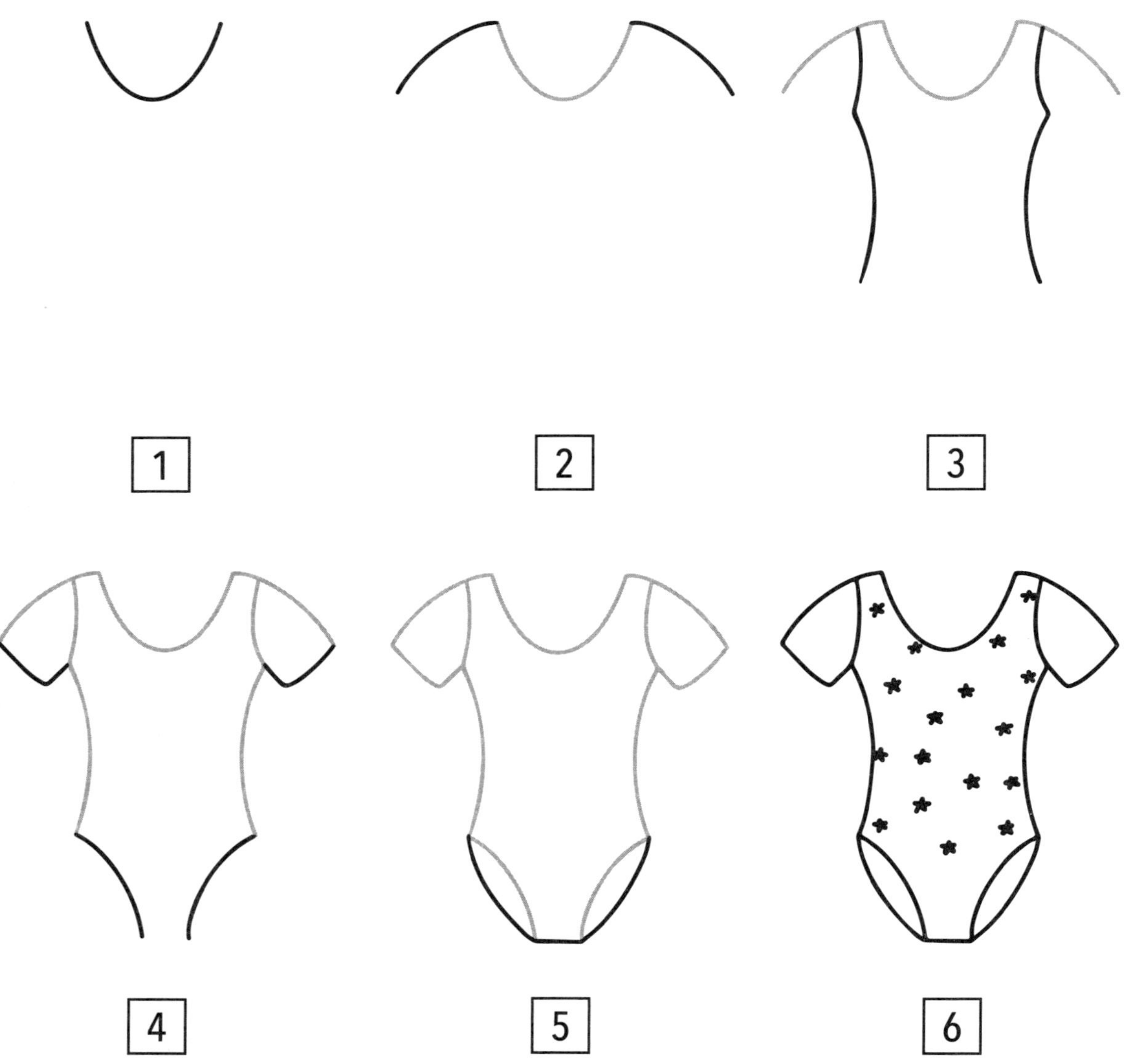

JERSEY

Professional team jerseys often include hidden details like team mottos, tiny logos, or secret symbols, tucked inside the collar or sleeves.

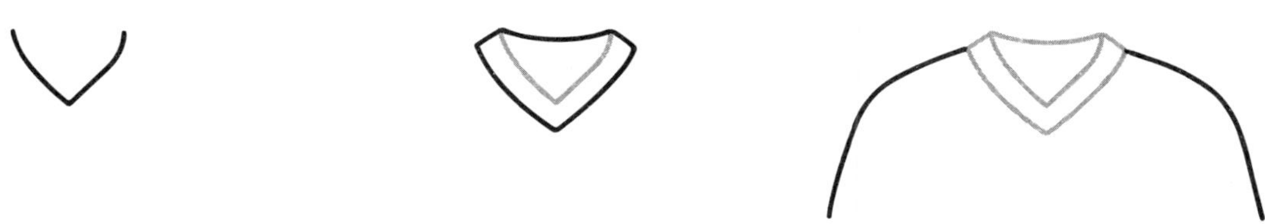

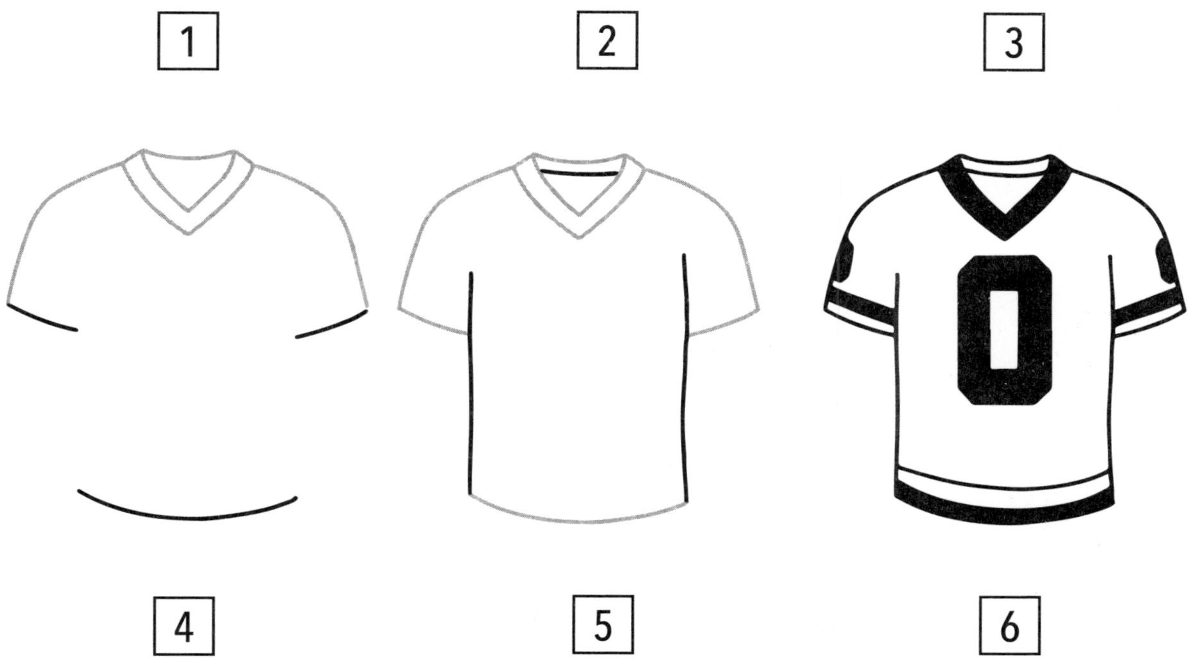

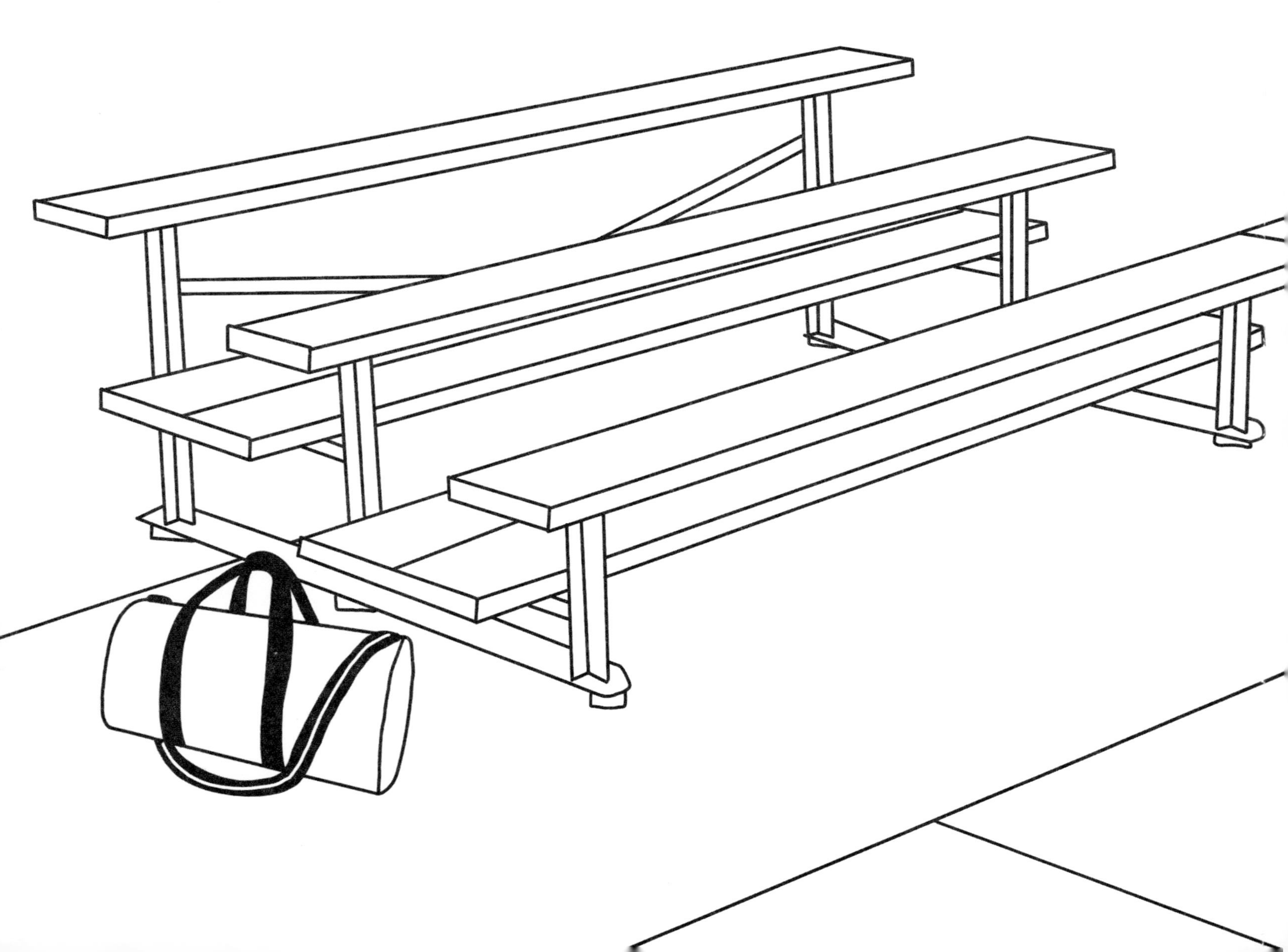

SPORTS ACCESSORIES

GYM BAG

Gym bags come in all shapes and sizes. Some have vents for stinky cleats, while others have pockets for rackets, balls, or baseball bats.

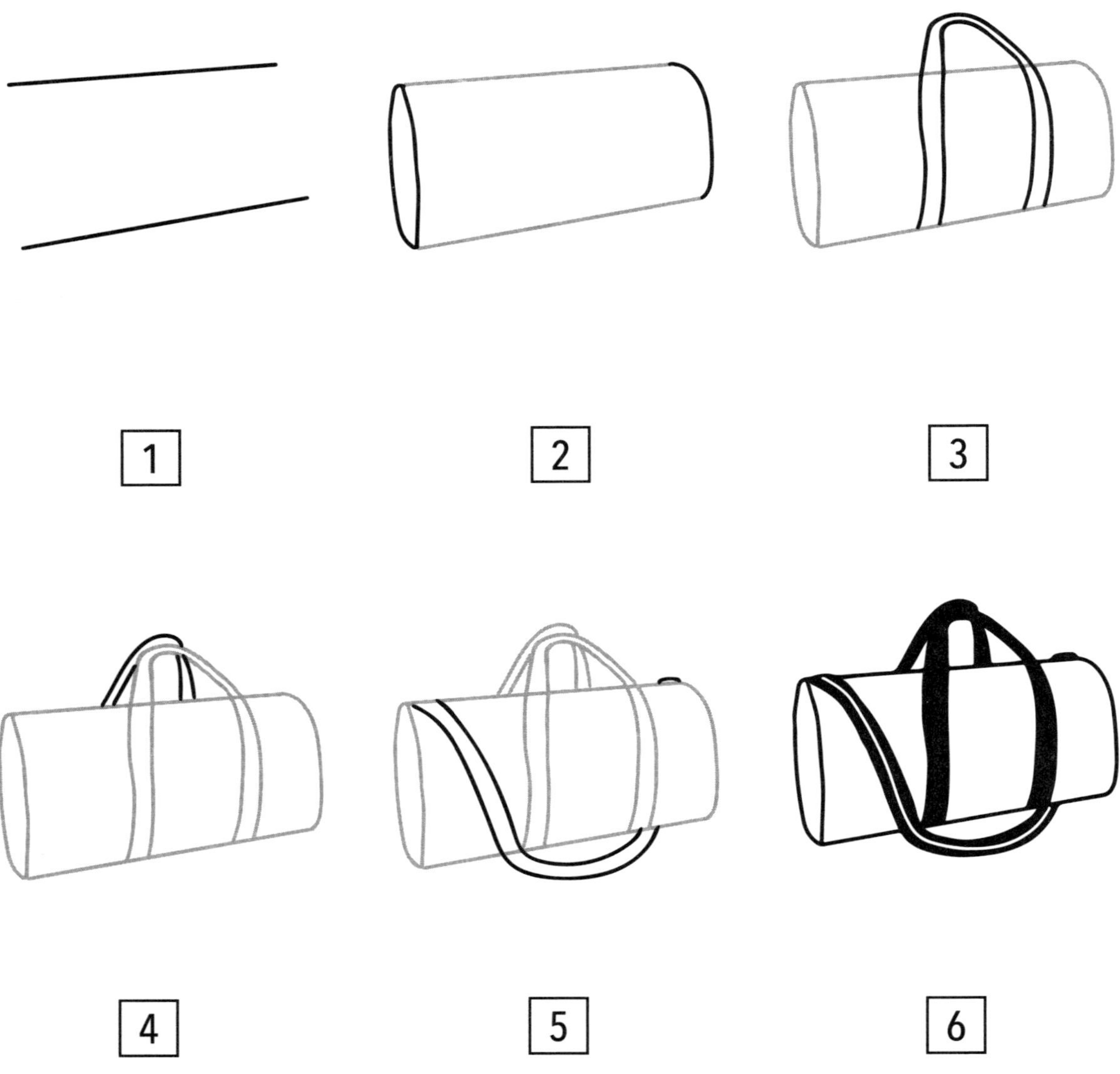

WATER BOTTLE

Most kids need 5–8 cups of water a day, but on hot days or after sports, you might need 10 cups or more to stay hydrated.

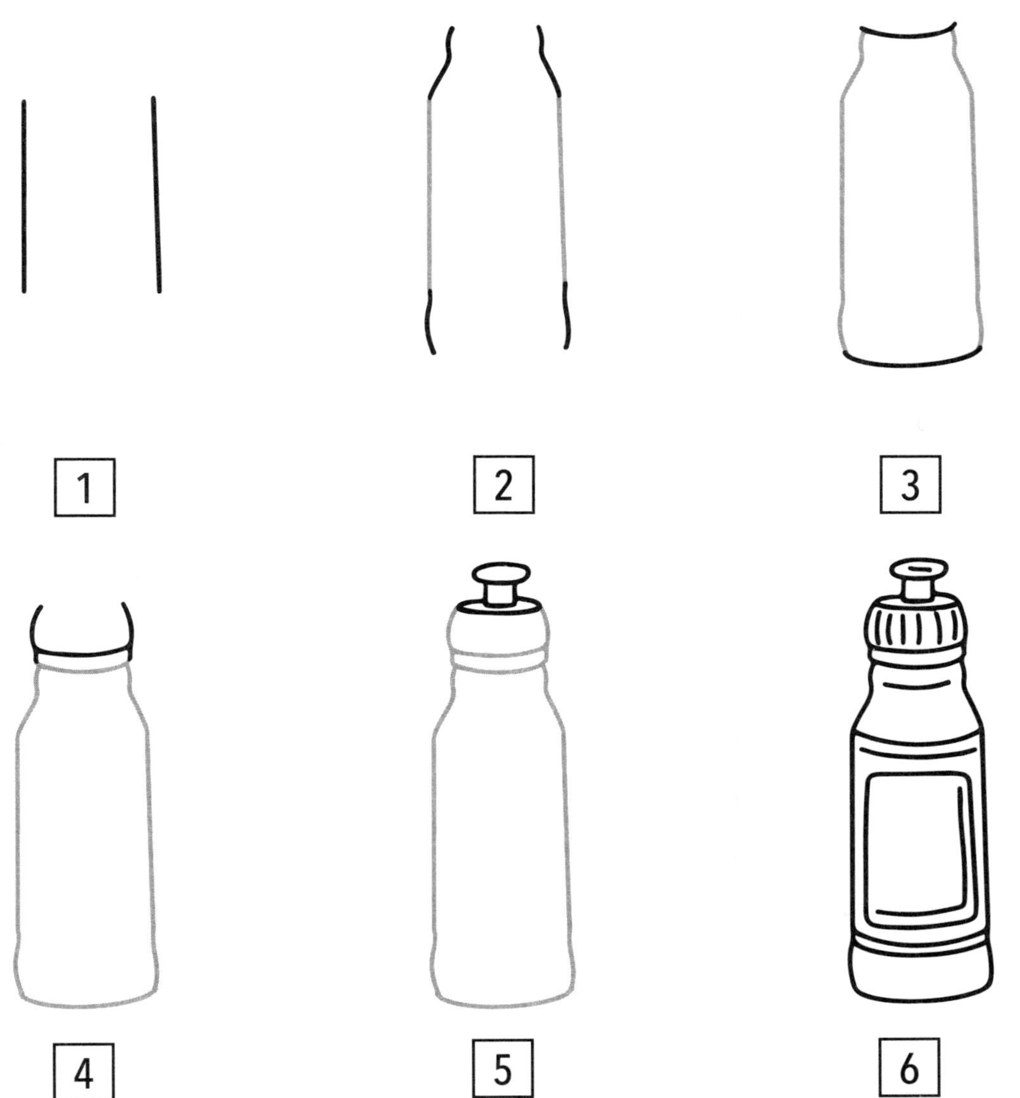

MEDAL

Olympic gold medals aren't made of solid gold. They're mostly made of silver with a thin layer of gold on the outside.

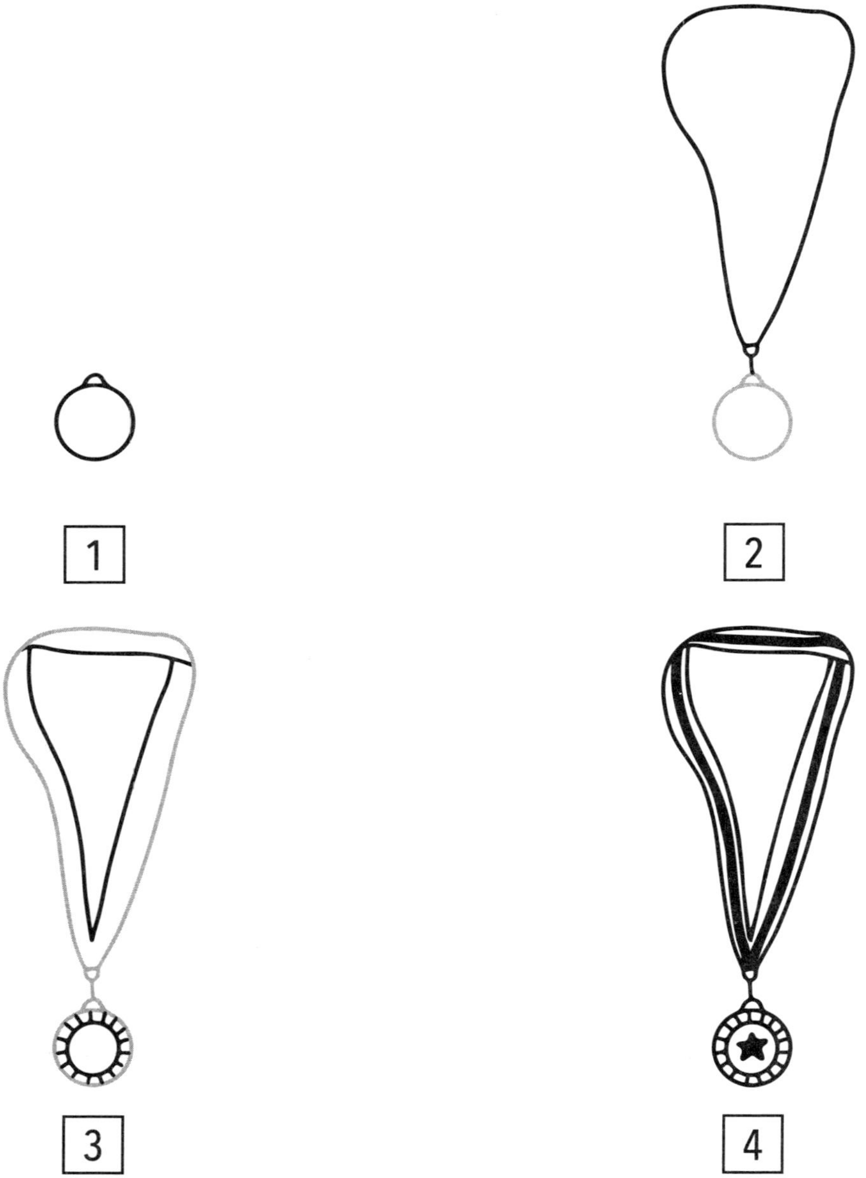

TROPHY

Modern metal and plastic trophies became popular in the 1950s. Before that, winners often received cups, plaques, or, in the first Olympic games, leafy wreaths.

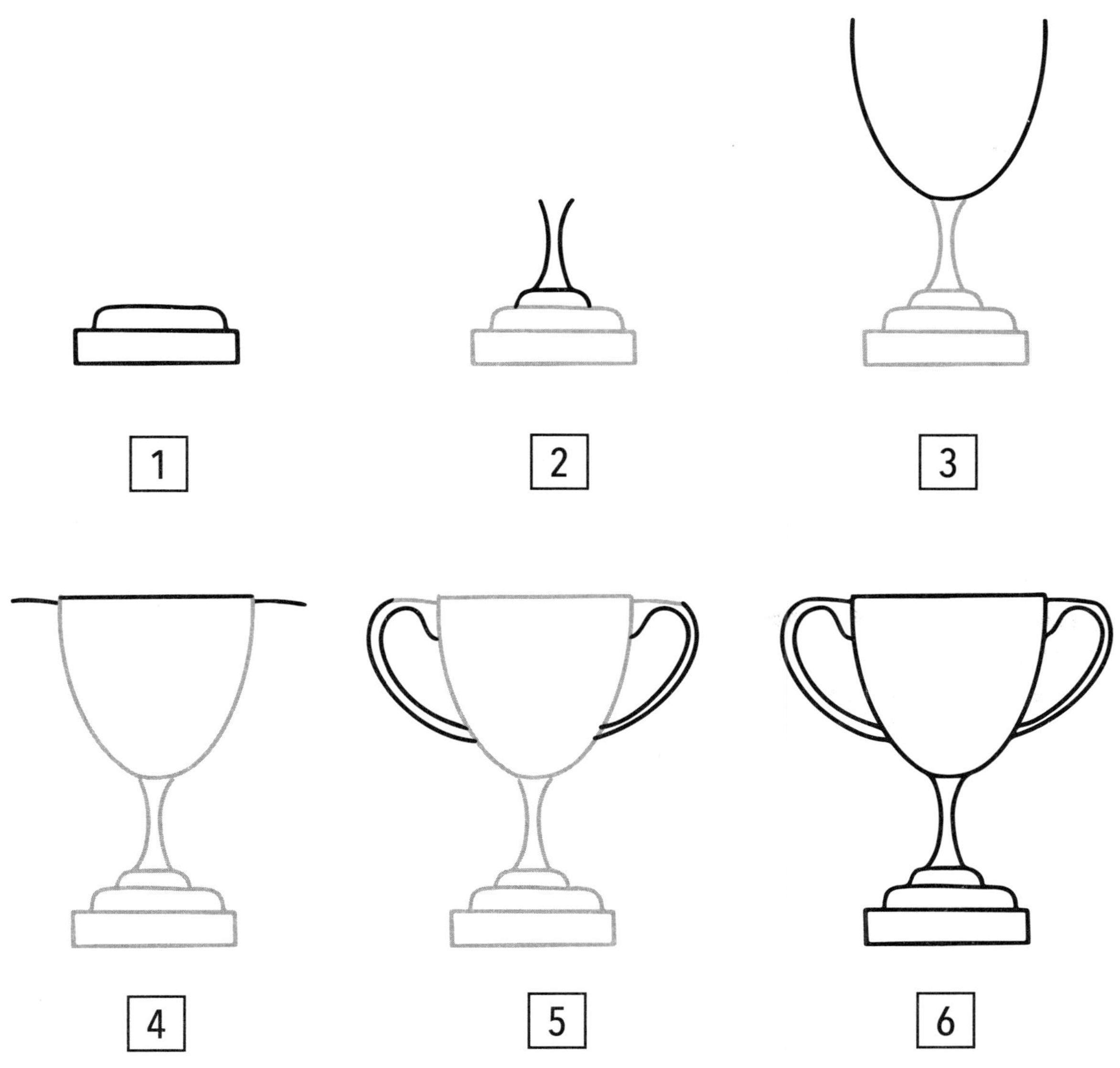

RIBBON

At horse shows, riders and horses can earn place ribbons in every color.
Blue is the best, but even a pink ribbon means you had a winning ride.

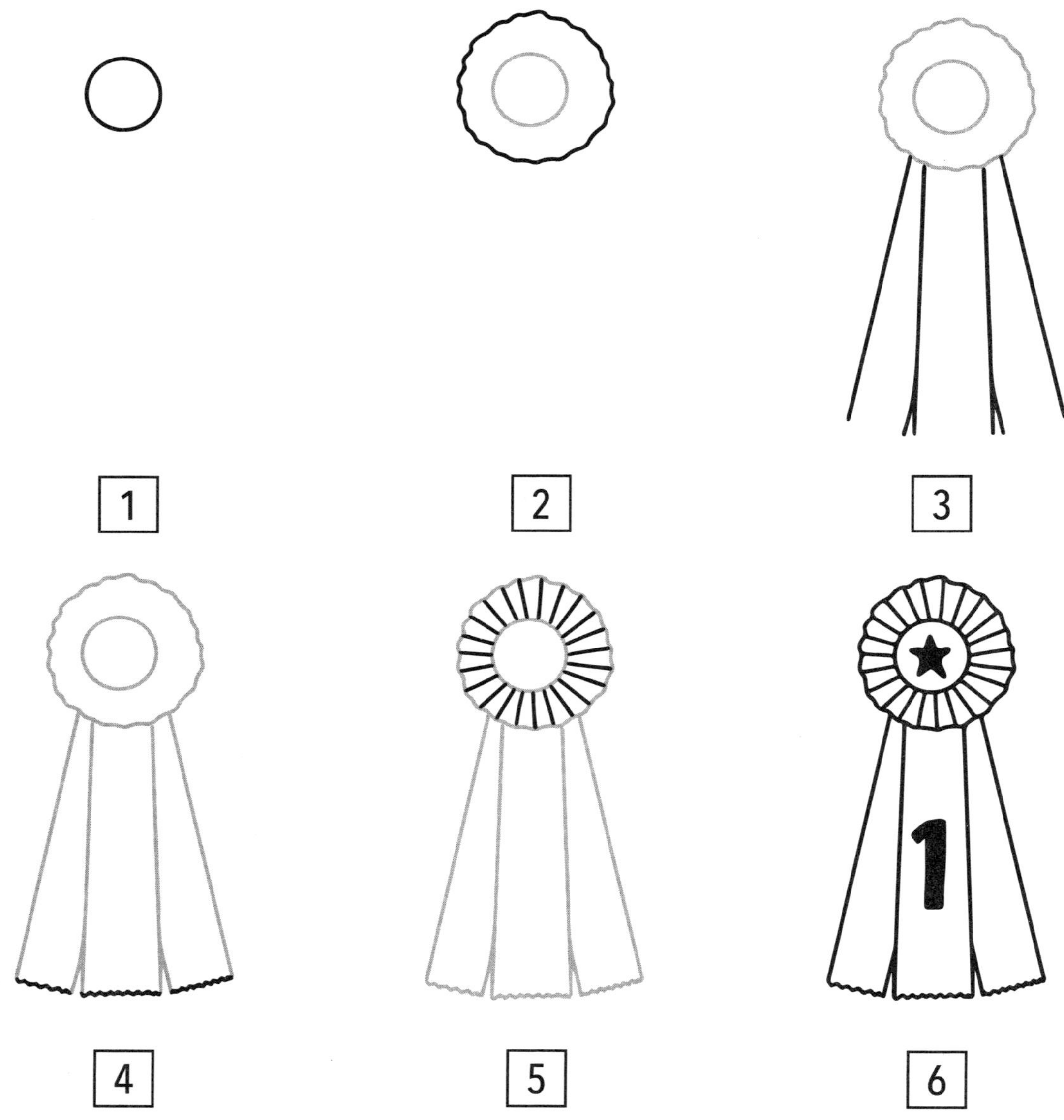

MEGAPHONE

Cheerleading began in the 1880s with all-male "yell leaders" at college football games who used giant wooden megaphones that doubled as drums.

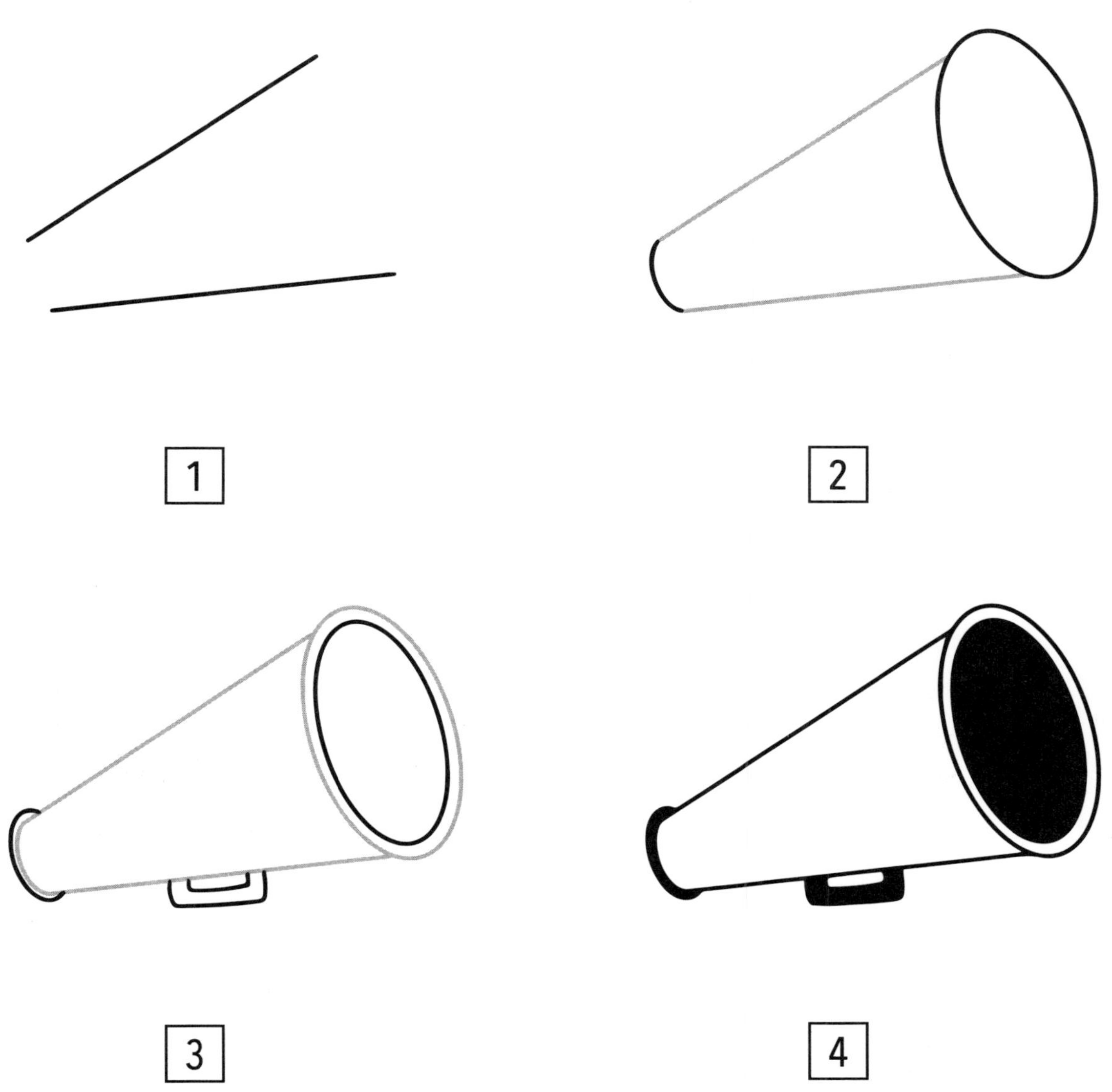

WHISTLE

Sports whistles can blast over 100 decibels—louder than some rock concerts!

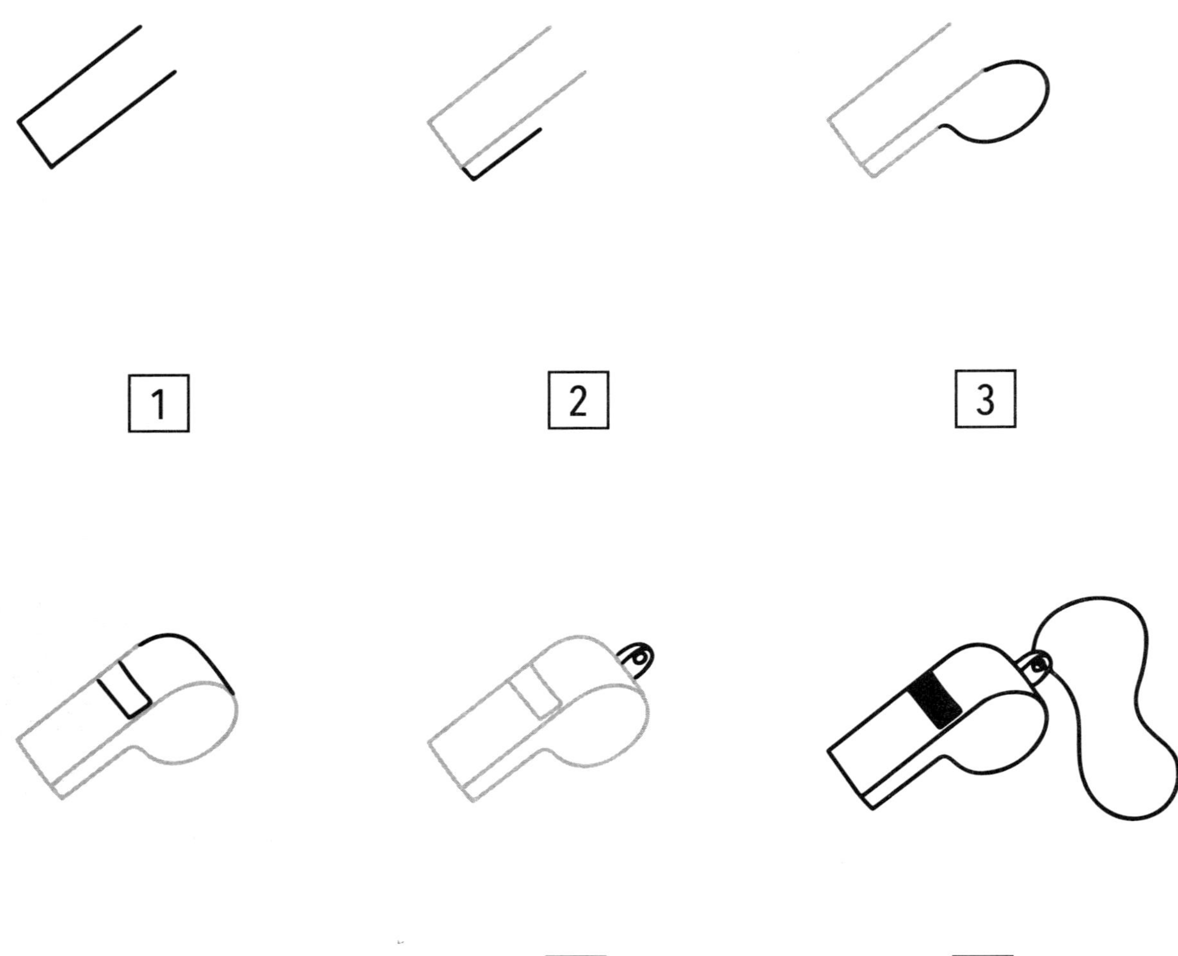

WEIGHT

Weight training helps all athletes get faster, stronger, and recover more quickly!

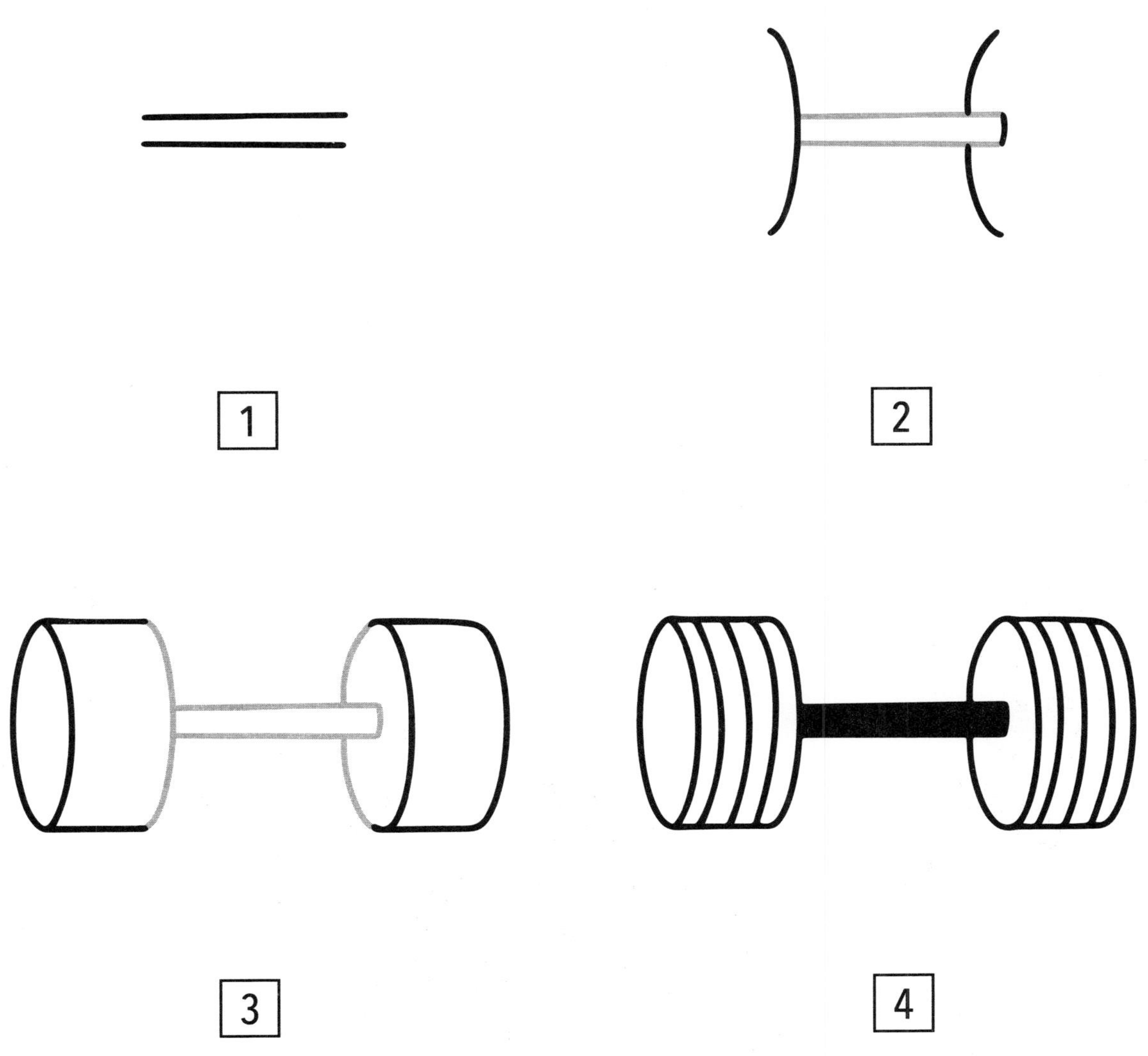

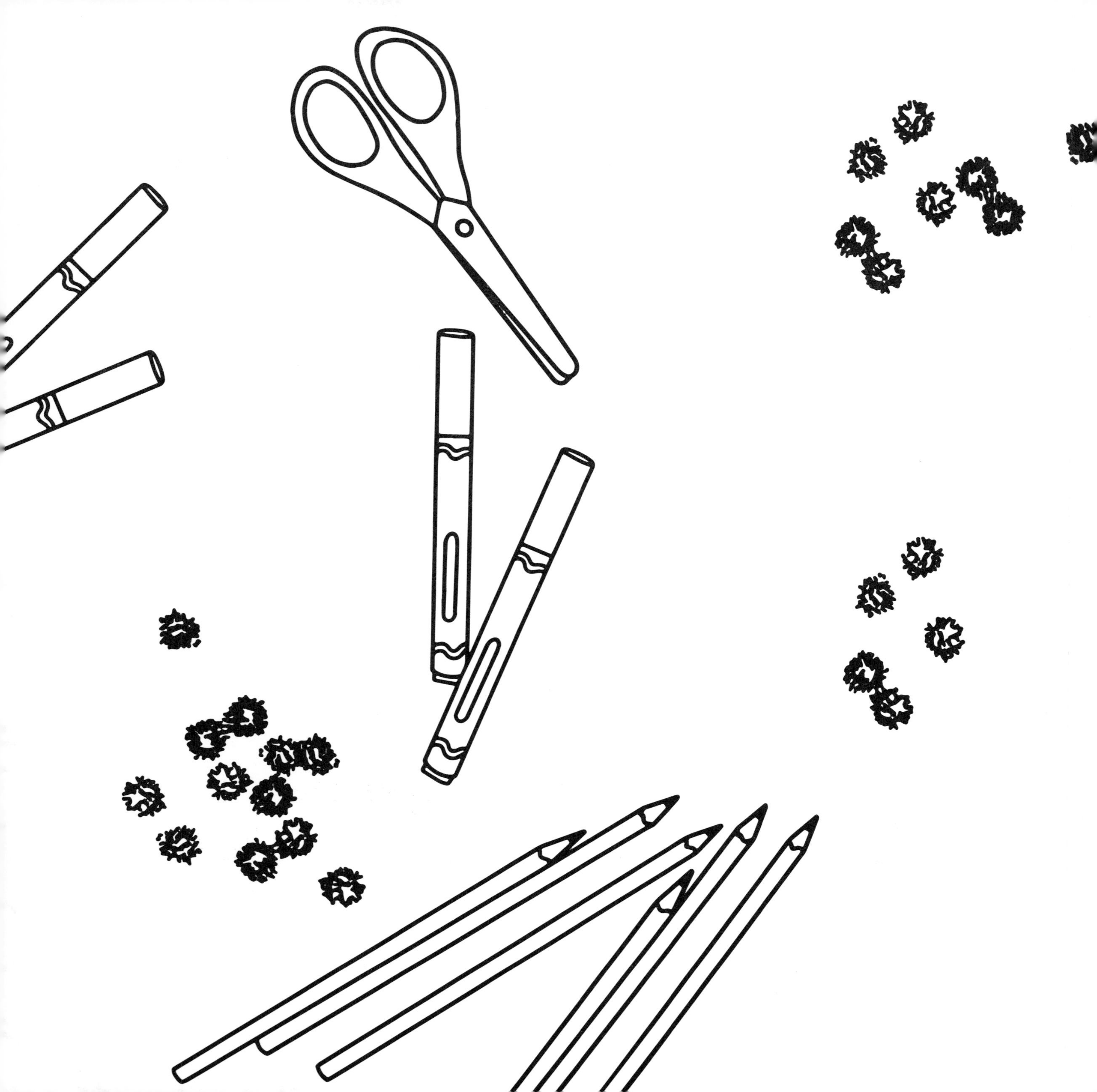

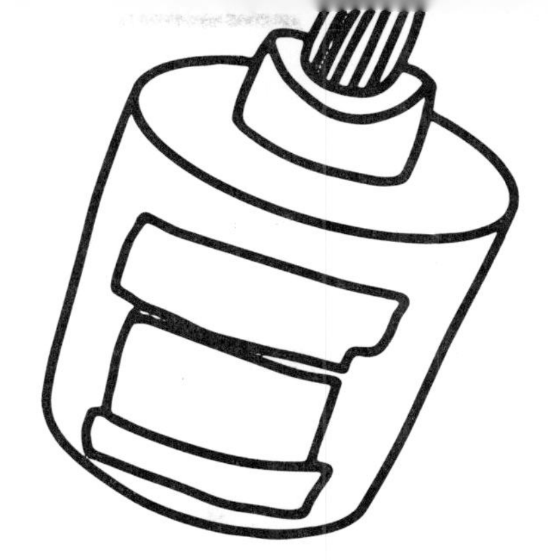

CREATE YOUR OWN

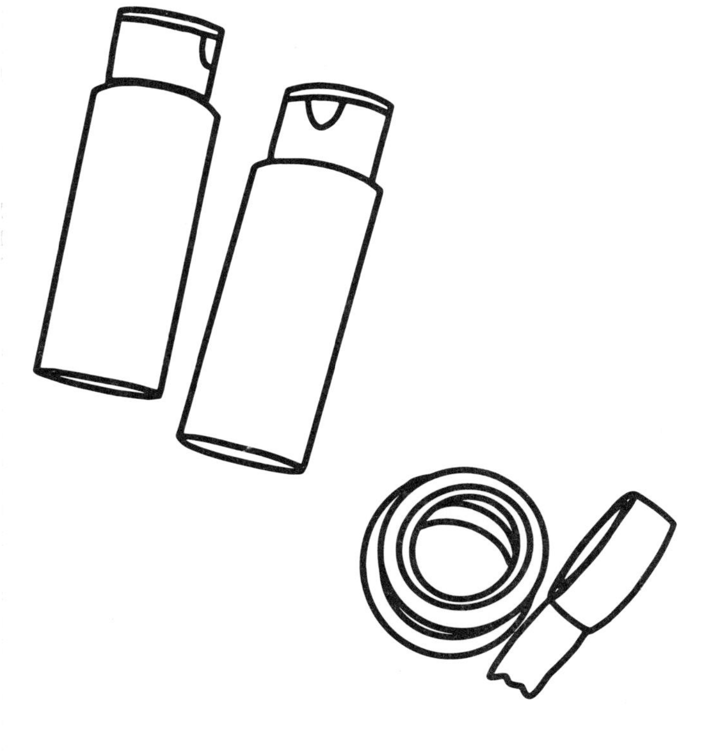

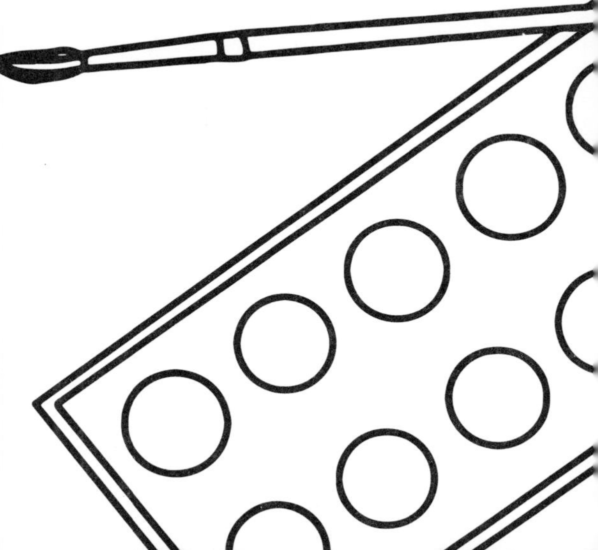

CREATE YOUR OWN JERSEY

Use this page to create a your own sports jersey!

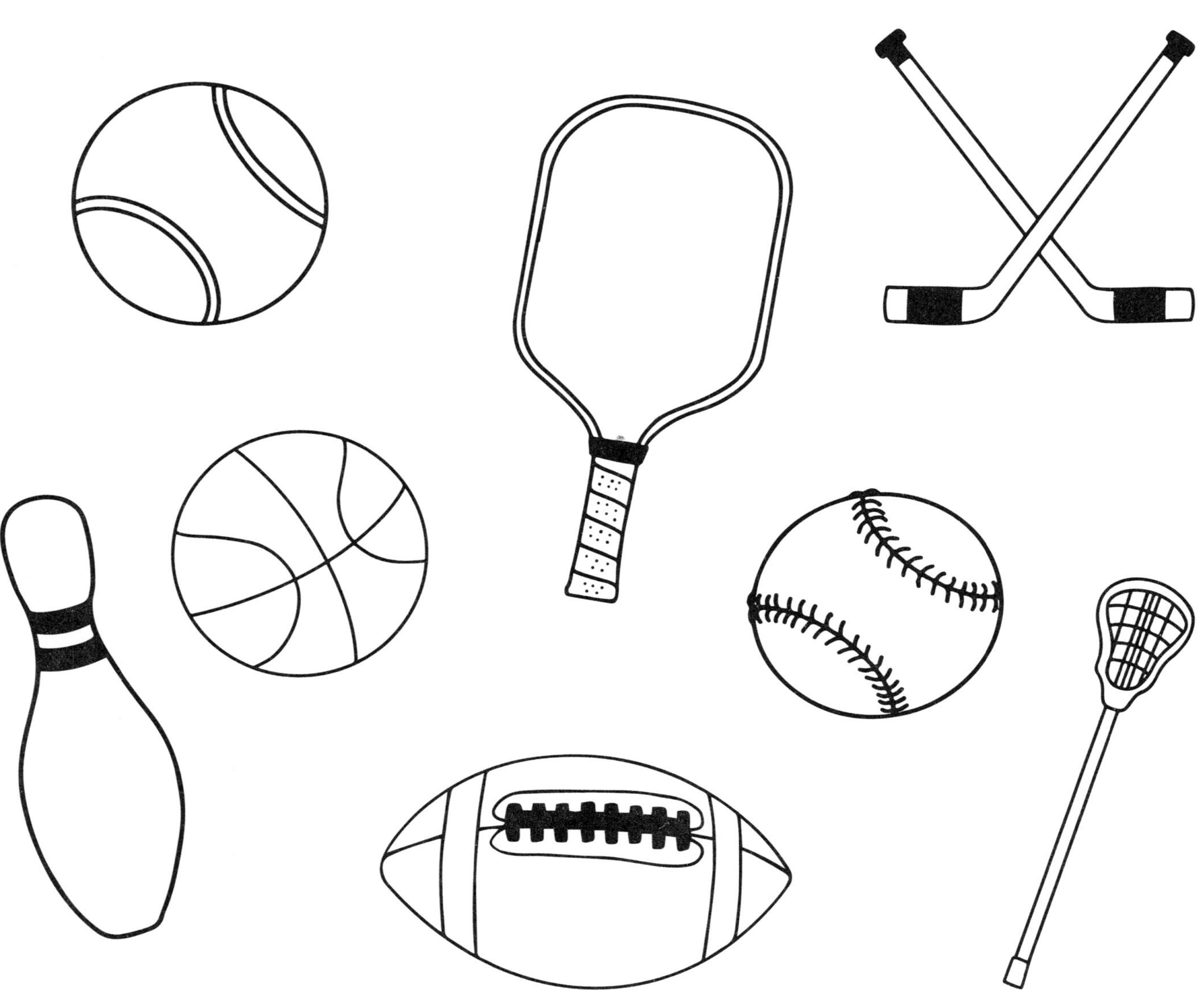

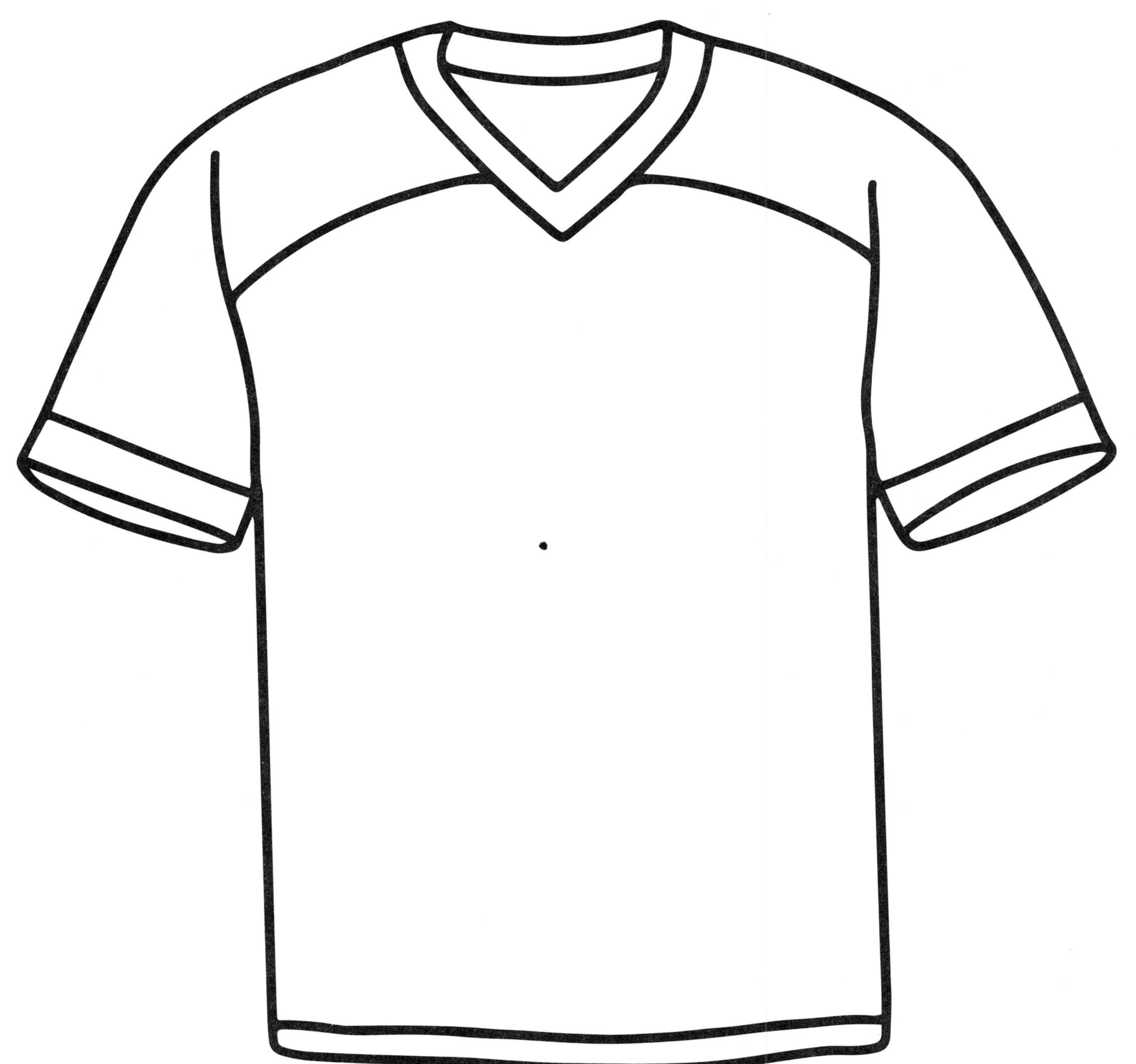

CREATE YOUR OWN AWARD

Use this page to draw your own sports award!

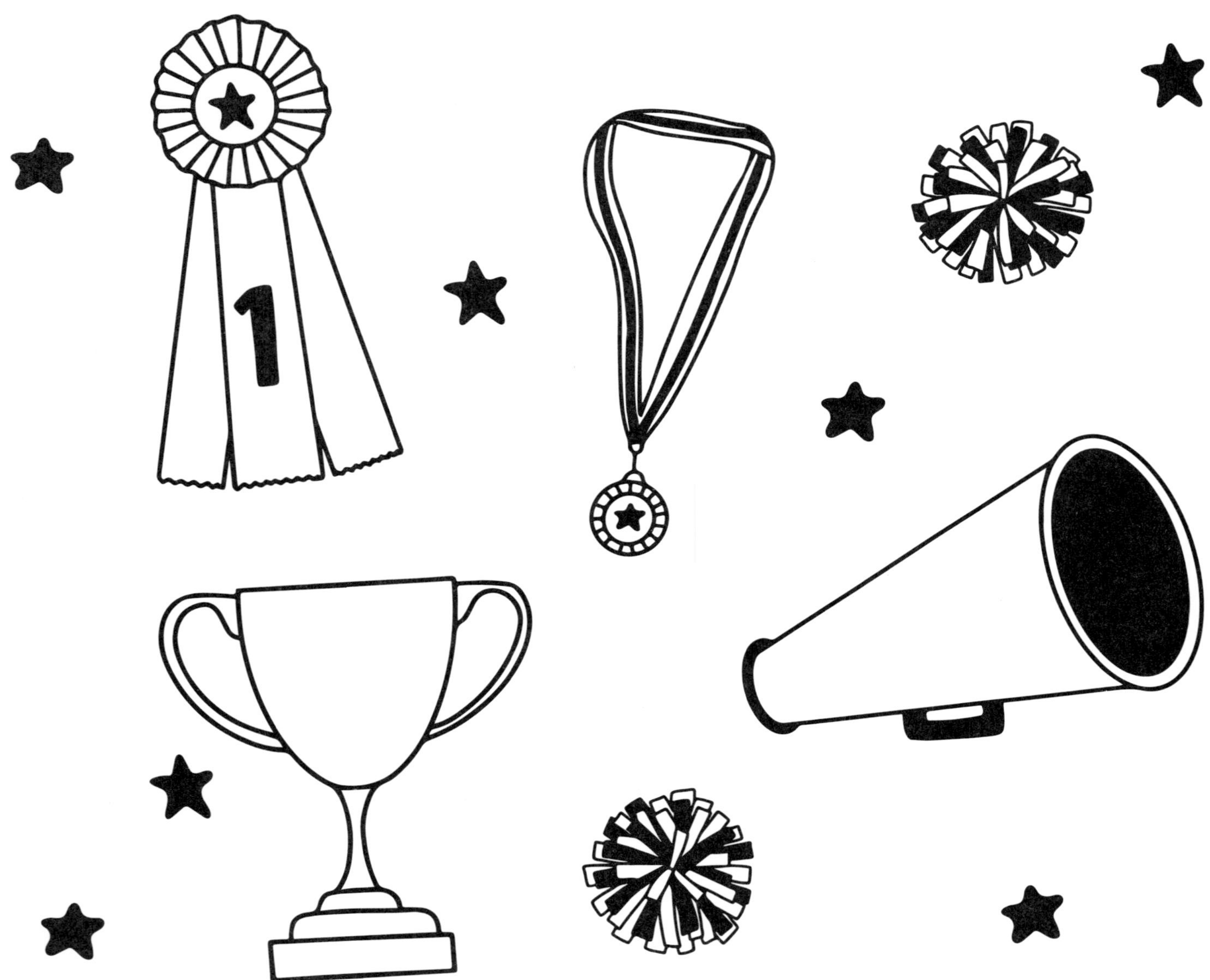

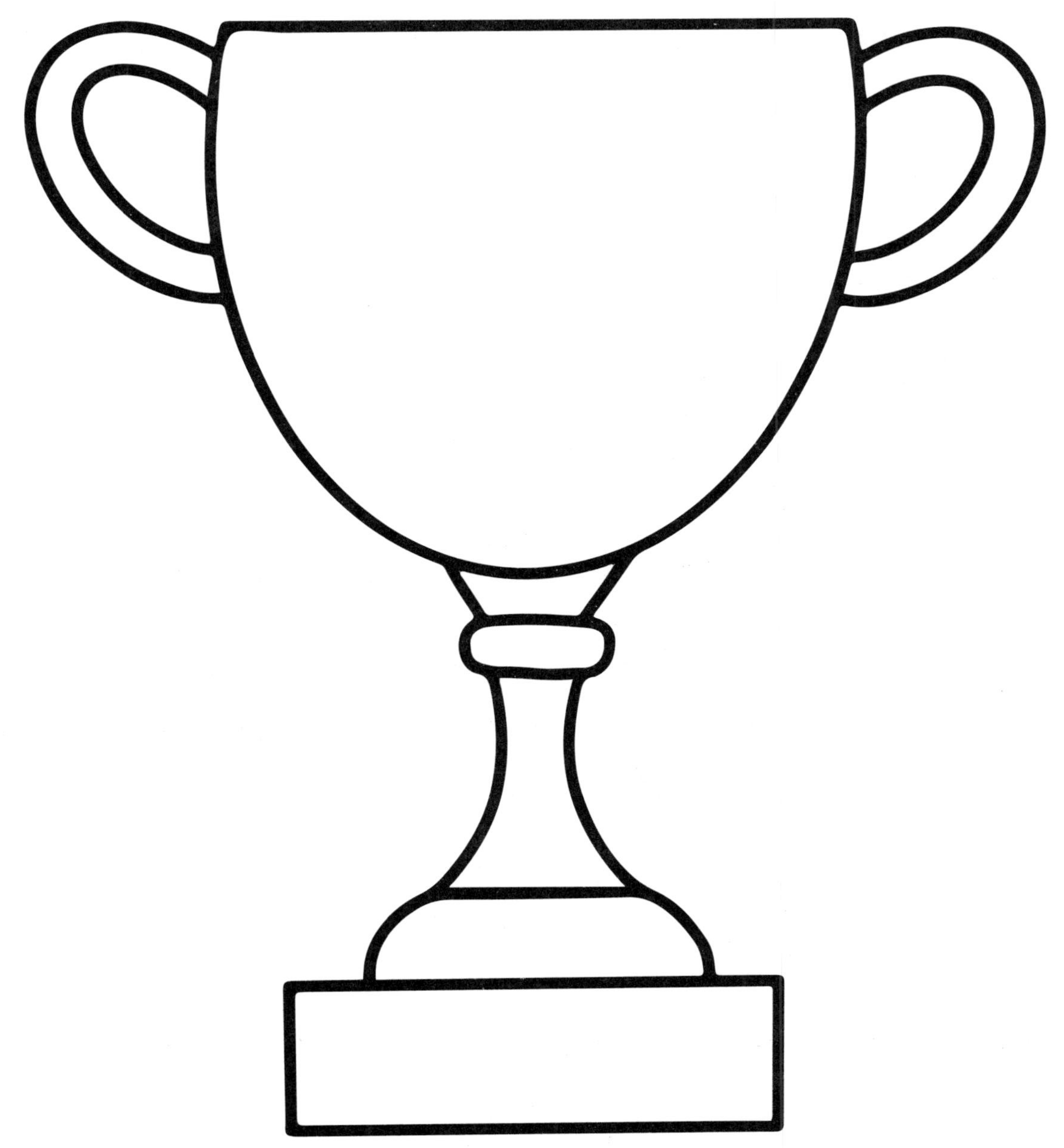

About Alli K

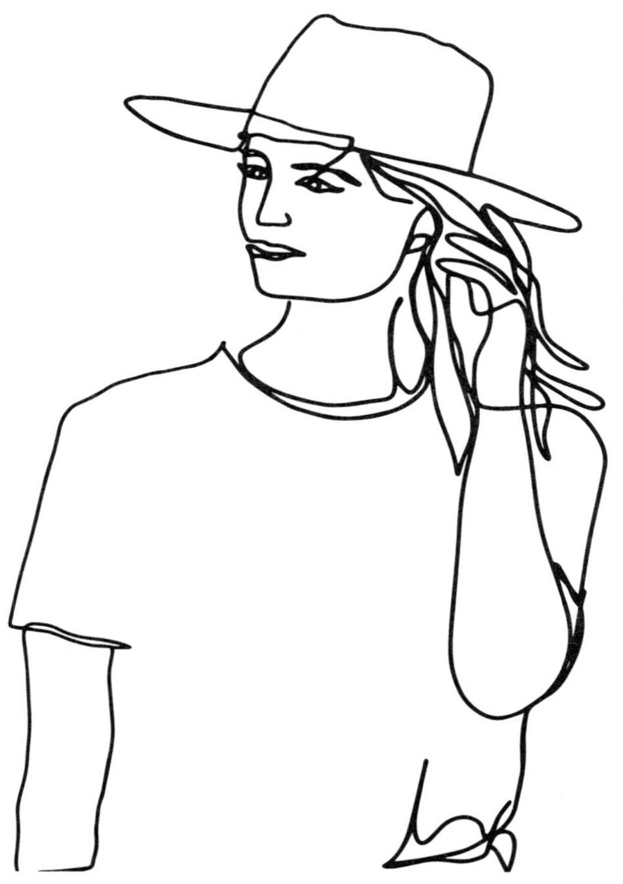

NAME: Alli Koch

HOME: Dallas, Texas

BIRTHDAY: March 20, 1991

FAVORITE COLOR: Black

FAVORITE FOOD: Waffle fries and a large sweet tea

JOB: I am a full-time artist! I sell my art online, paint murals on the side of buildings, and teach others how to draw or be creative.

FAVORITE SPORT: Cheerleading

PETS: I have two cats named Emmie and Bex

CAR: Two-door Jeep

FAMILY: Married to my high school sweetheart

FAVORITE THING TO DO: Play board games!

LOVE TO DRAW? COLLECT THE WHOLE *HOW TO DRAW FOR KIDS* SERIES!

- All the Things
- All the Magical Things
- All the Animals
- Modern Flowers
- Under the Sea
- Woodland Creatures
- Spring Things
- Summer Things
- Fall Things
- Winter Things